mixed

blessings

PAULA RIPPLE COMIN

ave maria press Notre Dame, Indiana

© 1999 by Ave Maria Press, Inc.

International Standard Book Number: 0-87793-666-8

Cover and text design by Katherine Robinson Coleman

Printed and bound in the United States of America.

Library of Congress Cataloging-in-Publication Data

Comin, Paula Ripple.
        Mixed blessings / Paula Ripple Comin.
                    p.   cm.
        ISBN 0-87793-666-8
        1. Christian life—Catholic authors.   I. Title.
BX2350.2.C61325   1999
248.4—dc21

                                                            98-37485
                                                            CIP

For our sons,

Scott, the actor,

and

Chris, the civil engineer,

with loving thanks

for your faithfulness

to your own lives.

Contents

Acknowledgments

I view my life as a piece of work that is, primarily, my own. I have tried to respond faithfully to God's persistent grace and the ever-present call to grow beyond where I am comfortable. I am deeply grateful to those who have loved me unconditionally and encouraged me along the way. Among those important to my present chapter of the journey are:

- ▼ My best friend and husband, Don Comin, whose presence makes life's mysterious project more loving, more challenging, and a whole lot more fun.
- ▼ The children at the shelters for battered women in LaCrosse, Wisconsin, and Naples, Florida, who, over the past eight years, have enriched my life by sharing with me their tears, their fears, their laughter, and their wonderful artwork that adorns my refrigerator.
- ▼ Frank and Sue Cunningham, who have been there for me through the writing of five books but, much more, through the most important transitions in my life.
- ▼ Leonard Hernandez, my teacher and friend, whose patience and wisdom have taught me much more than the essentials of the game of golf.
- ▼ All of my family and friends whose tested love knew only one season, the season of faithfulness.

Introduction

Welcome to a world of blessings reconsidered, unintended journeys lived through, barely. Welcome to reflections on the turmoil and tension we sometimes experience in the face of the chaos that inevitably follows in the wake of change.

The pages that follow reveal the growing edges of my life together with the lives of friends who have trusted me with the inner geography and mystery of their lives.

The following reflections represent some life themes that are significant to me and to people with whom I have shared the journey over the past several years.

Each chapter, though complete in itself, is a part of a larger pattern that can emerge through important connections between the various themes of this book.

It is hoped that part of the richness of this book will be found in the interfacing of key insights and the mixing of experiences with which each of us can identify.

Sometimes life speeds toward us in such a way that we only get out of the way and let it happen. But, at a later time, we may become curious about what happened, and we may search through remaining memories to discover the meaning that lies waiting to be recognized. This process is much like walking on a beach looking for shells until a particular one attracts our attention.

This inner process of searching for meaning can be the source of life's richest and most refined insights. It is the way in which hitherto hidden meaning surfaces, where sadness and turmoil give way to peace and understanding.

For this process to occur, we must have a commitment to the inward journey of which Dag Hammarskjöld spoke when he said that "the longest journey is the journey inward." It requires of us a willingness to leave the comfort of the margins in exchange for the costly still point at the center.

It is an energizing, humbling, and sometimes frightening experience to have been witness to people who discovered some important meaning for their lives simply by sharing a story one more time, with me. When this happens, I am profoundly moved but have never been tempted to believe that the sharing and the trust were because I am some sort of special person. To the extent that others have trusted me with their sacred places and spaces is related to the truth of my own struggles and disappointments as I have found words through which to share them. Through some painful beginnings and endings, when I questioned my own ability to survive and grow, these same events have often come to appear as blessings without which new life would not have been possible. The sometimes tough and tender love of God and friends helps me now to name these mixed blessings as the poet does, "dear bought victories."

Recently, as I was writing, I said to a wonderful friend, "Without this tragedy in your life, I would never have received the gift of your friendship."

Years ago a suicidal young woman said to me, "I hate you. You've never cared about me," even as she continued to depend on me in significant ways until she did, tragically and dramatically, end this troubled earthly phase of her journey.

A loved friend, thirty years old, exacted a promise of me to deliver the eulogy at his funeral, which was scarcely six months later. He asked me to promise that, out of sensitivity to his family, I mention neither homosexuality nor AIDS. I was free to speak of love and courage.

A prison pen pal shared with me his feelings about his "wasted life" and the grim climate that exists among his fellow prisoners. Through his letters and the sharing of an autobiography that he hopes to have published, I found myself as a traveler in a world much larger than it was when I received his first letter several years ago.

I continually challenge him to seek an inner freedom that no prison walls can take from him.

A young woman agonized over an unwanted pregnancy and the absence of the father. Having made the decision to have the baby, she also looked ahead to giving up the baby for adoption because she believed that she was not emotionally mature enough to provide appropriate parenting alone.

A woman housed in a shelter had a heart attack and

had to give up her work as the caretaker of two men dying of AIDS. She found herself robbed of the one thing giving meaning to her life.

These sacred human stories are reminders to me of my own mixed blessings and experiences through which I have been challenged far beyond my comfort level. When these and other human stories are mixed, they offer the mysterious awareness of formerly unnoticed hues that enrich the tapestry of life. No human life can reach its fullest meaning apart from life shared with others, apart from stories blended and refined.

Human lives are connected; they are also interconnected. With each life, the pieces of personal history, the letters of each person's alphabet, tell a wondrous story and offer a tapestry rich in depth and meaning. One note cannot make a symphony, one lovely leaf is not a tree, one grain of sand is not a beach. One human life, apart from the mixing of blessings with other lives, will lack the luster it might have had.

> A crystal goblet is my soul
> In sacred cabinet's store
> A rainbow hidden in the whole
> and empty gleaming more.
> The paradox of heaven's mend
> Deciphered in this code:
> Shattered into sparkling pieces
> Only truth shared in brokenness releases
> Beauty deeper still.

▼ FRANKLIN L. BARTEL

Life as Journey: The Canyon Gorge Chapter

> *We cannot begin with the celebration—we arrive at the ability to celebrate by way of a journey.*
>
> ▼ CARL JUNG

I remember well my first journey to Canyon Gorge. It was in August of 1991.

I was met at the Phoenix airport by a staff member at the conference center who asked me if I had ever been to Canyon Gorge. I told her that I not only had not been there, but that I couldn't find it on any map.

She smiled and said simply, "You are about to make a journey into an incredibly beautiful canyon. You will find few places that can equal what you will see."

I have never forgotten her words. Their meaning deepened for me through the next several years as I made the same journey each fall and winter to help direct a workshop related to discovering and seeking healing for our broken places.

Canyon Gorge has become a lasting symbol of the Christian journey, and of the relentless pursuit of a God whose love is as lavish as it is challenging.

The canyon, in which this now sacred place is nestled, reminded me of an image of *The Hand of God* sculpted by the Swedish artist John Milles. The artist's symbol reminds us that God's hand supports us, holds us, sets us free, does not seek to restrain us, and remains with us.

At the same time, God's hand, because it is freeing, invites us to approach life with open arms and hearts and challenges us to let go of what is self-destructive, even as it invites us to catch hold of some new form of life that is continually being offered. Few who have seen this sculpture in Stockholm could ever forget the figure resting in a hand atop a very tall pillar.

In that canyon, and wending its way through the complex of buildings which is the conference center, is a river. At times, when the water level is low, it is possible to forget that the river is there—so gentle is its song and movement.

At other times, the river rushes along with such forcefulness and with such great volume that you can hear its song as you drop off to sleep at night.

I feel blessed to have continued to be invited to return to this incredibly beautiful place twice a year. As the women and men shared their life stories with me, I was reminded of the words of Carl Jung about our inability to begin with the celebration.

I became more convinced of my belief that all life is either born or strengthened through some form of suffering. I also believe that personal decision plays a unique role in whether or not we ever come to the time and place of celebration.

I discovered that a part of the journey to the canyon was reflected in a Bob Dylan song/story. As the Dylan story goes, three men are desirous of finding the cave of wisdom and life. So great is their intent that they eventually set out on what proves to be a long and arduous journey. Because of the many unexpected obstacles along the way, they are forced to rely on one another for support and even survival.

One can only imagine their joy and relief when, one day, they see what they believe to be the entrance to the cave only a short distance from them. They approach with eagerness, wishing to enter the cave immediately. Instead, as they come closer, they see a guard watching over the entrance.

As they arrive at the entrance, one of the three asks, "Is this the cave of wisdom and life?"

When the man at the entrance replies that it is, they advance as if to enter immediately. They are surprised when he steps into their path and says, "If you wish to enter this cave, there is one question you must answer. You must tell me, 'How far into the cave of wisdom and life do you wish to go?'"

The three men step back to take counsel together. After some deliberation, the spokesman steps forward.

The guard asks again, "How far into the cave of wisdom and life do you wish to go?"

The response of the three is, "Oh, not very far. Just far enough so that we can say that we have been here."

In the light of their prior commitment to the journey, and the difficulty they had in arriving there, the response seems disappointing. One is mystified at their seeming superficiality. One wonders about their reasons for ever setting out in the first place.

The meaning of the story was renewed for me as I continued to return to Canyon Gorge, for I came to see this lovely canyon as a "cave of wisdom and life." It is a place to which men and women come who have experienced themselves needing both healing and hope. It is a place in which the same essential question is put to each workshop participant, "How deeply do you wish to enter into your own journey, and into the challenges being offered to you here?"

I remember asking those in workshop sessions, "Can a person come here and remain unchanged?"

It is in and through our brokenness that we can become convinced that there is a God whose unfailing love for us cannot be lost, who created us whole and waits for us to discover the fullness of life.

It was an added gift for me that I made the journey into the canyon at varying points when these searching women and men were there. I was sometimes there very early in the program, shortly after the painful yet beautiful sharing of each one's personal journey. At this early time, it was not uncommon for someone to tell me how angry she was that she needed a place like this—feeling more broken than whole.

When I was there to share the middle portion of their journey, the workshop was seen as an experience of some kind of synthesis for them—a coming together of some of the seemingly disjointed pieces.

If I was there near the end of the program, they commonly spoke of the gift dimension of having been somehow planted in God's hand to be nurtured and encouraged, to be supported and set free.

Many of the participants told me that never in their lives had they experienced such a sense of being deeply respected and cared about; never before had they felt so strongly the *presence* of others who shared their vulnerability and their hope. For many, it was their first experience of real family, of true community.

It was as though they were coming close to celebrating the unfolding of their own precious lives. Jung's words proved to be true—their journey did not begin with the celebration.

I do not know if a man or woman could leave Canyon Gorge unchanged. I do know that I did not: I feel richer and deeper for having been privileged to share a part of the journey with such good men and women. I feel deeply grateful to those who shared their lives with me in ways which were, I believe, mutually enriching and life-giving. Leaving them and the sacred place of the canyon was never easy.

Knowing that my role was as a transition person for those who were there as they decided how deeply they wanted to enter into their personal cave of wisdom and life, I left the canyon for the final time, several years after my first visit, remembering the words of Morris West in *The Clowns of God*: "We've met most powerfully at the crossroads. We'll part, each a little richer."

We Belong to Each Other

We live in an age of rapid change. It is an age of unparalleled possibility. It is an age when millions feel closer to a dear-bought human freedom from oppressive systems of government.

In such times, people reach for the fulfillment of their dreams for a better way of life. At these times, people rediscover that the costs of such dreams have never been cheap.

In such times, people discover that they are somehow bonded to all who have shared their own or a similar journey. The words of St. Paul reveal the same message: "For as in one body we have many parts, and all the parts do not have the same function, so we, though many, are one body in Christ and individually parts of one another" (Rom 12:4-5).

In such times, thoughtful people wonder where the leadership should come from that is required if we are not to give way to the forces of chaotic oppression and unbridled impatience.

There is need for new structures that are faithful to the quest for freedom and responsibility set in the human heart by God who loves us and calls us to the richness of human life. How shall these new structures emerge?

And, in this time, we read the following words:

> Consciousness precedes being, and not the other way around. . . . For this reason, the salvation of this human world lies nowhere else than in the human heart, in the power to reflect, in human meekness, and in human responsibility.

> We are still incapable of understanding that the only genuine backbone of all our actions, if they are to be moral, is responsibility . . . responsibility to the order of being where all our actions are indelibly recorded and where, and only where, they will be properly judged.

They are the words of Vaclav Havel, the president of the former Czechoslovakia, in an address delivered to the Congress of the United States. They are words that emerge from the fertile soil of a human heart whose convictions deepened through the seventeen years he spent in a communist prison.

Havel's words bring much more than inspiration. They evoke strong hopefulness about the future of the human family as we go into the new millennium. They provide support as we discover cultural currents rich in their unique possibility of offering a better quality of life for all.

Havel's words offer a challenge to each of us. They invite us to become more aware of the changes in the world around us. His words challenge us to be more faithful to the inward journey into our own hearts.

SOME INCREASINGLY APPARENT CULTURAL CURRENTS IN OUR TIME

The emergence of greater awareness of the connectedness of all things. Environmentalists are reminding us in ever more factual and all-encompassing ways of some basic truths about our world.

We face serious questions about environmental problems that threaten even our continued existence. We are being forced to acknowledge that our carelessness about the planet on which we live cannot be allowed to continue.

Daily we read in our newspapers of the gravity of our attitudes toward waste disposal that threatens our lives as we pillage our earth, air, and water.

As we hear more talk about recycling, about our need to change our consumerist ways, we are called to a greater awareness of the countless ways in which our decisions and actions influence the lives of people who live far away.

We are receiving some powerful invitations to become people of prayer and self-reflection, people who believe that we are responsible for the earth, and for each other.

When we grow more and more aware of the many

ways in which our lives touch the lives of others, we will understand an ancient Aztec prayer:

> Oh, only for so short a while
> have you loaned us to each other.
> Because we take form in your act drawing us,
> and we breathe in your singing us.
> Because you have loaned us to each other.

The emergence of the age of the individual. We speak of the individual as a person of responsibility, a person who understands the eastern dogma of karma—"Every action generates consequences that the actor will eventually face."

It is of the *individual* that we speak, not the individualist.

The *individual* seeks to identify and to be part of life at the center; the individualist seeks the security of the margins.

The *individual* is willing to invest in the life of the human community; the individualist is self-centered.

The *individual* is willing to carry the responsibility for the life of many; the individualist carries the concern for an isolated issue.

How to explain the movements toward freedom in Poland, Czechoslovakia, China, and South Africa, among many others? The explanation is the courage of *individuals* who came together, strengthened by the roots of a faith that is deep and a vision of the future which sought the good of the many and not just of the few.

In other ways, through many forms of self-help

groups and neighborhood coalitions, through prayer groups and small faith communities, we can take hope in the faith-filled life that grows more apparent.

We can take hope from the realization that the age of individualism is also past for nations as we speak of "common markets," "world banks," and multinational efforts.

The emergence of the awareness that the greatest power in the universe is the power that resides deep within the human spirit—the inner power of the universe. Jesus often reminded us that the "kingdom is within" (Lk 17:21). The world in which we live has lost sight of that important truth. We have looked to nuclear warheads, to wealth, to governmental structures as the most important places of power. We could not only "rule" the world, but make decisions for everyone else on earth.

We are reminded that the most profound changes in our world happen not through the force of guns. Rather, these changes result from the courage and the human spirit of people of faith responding to the call of a Creator God to seek truth and freedom.

A new kind of life is emerging. In the face of such great change, responsible people can no longer remain indifferent.

HOPE LIES IN THE RESPONSE THAT EACH OF US MAKES

Above all, the new millennium can be a time of great hope. The key to the future is to be found in the human heart. The source of energy lies in the willingness of each person to accept the profound invitation to explore his or her own inner space with the same creativity and commitment as we have explored outer space.

The words of Vaclav Havel and the cultural trends described above are reminders of the need for prayer. They are reminders of the need to take time to look inward, so that we may reach out to others with greater respect and sensitivity.

Every one of us is called to take the time and make the effort required to heal our own hurts, to have our own wounds bound up. The process of personal healing brings with it a unique kind of strength and a renewed sense of hope. Paradoxically, this process of personal healing intensifies our desire that others may be healed and freed of whatever chains bind them.

As each of us finds an appropriate way to respond to the call of our time, we will come to discover the new and deeper meaning of the words of St. Paul when he says so simply, "We belong to each other."

Forgiveness: A Way to Healing and Life

There is a powerful scene in the classic film *A Tale of Two Cities*. An old grandfather is found hiding in an attic. He is suffering from malnutrition and seems close to death.

When he is asked how he feels about the perpetrators of his great suffering, the old man ponders carefully and then responds:

> In suffering, one learns many things. One learns that it is important not to be responsible for deliberately bringing pain into the lives of others. One also learns that without a willingness to forgive those who have hurt us, it is not likely that our lives can go on in any meaningful manner. I do not wish to be a lifelong captive of my captors.

The old man's words are a reminder of Ghandi's attitude toward those who had brought much injustice and hardship to his people. He said, "Forgiveness is the virtue of the brave. He alone is strong enough to avenge a wrong who knows how to love and forgive."

The words of Ghandi and of the old man challenge us to remember that we are often involved in some aspect of either offering or seeking forgiveness. The decision we make about forgiveness will give shape and form to the kind of person we are becoming.

Jesus was serious when he said that seven times is not enough to forgive. "Seven times seventy times" was what Jesus suggested.

Words that are used often sometimes lose their power for us. Words like *love, respect, care* and *forgiveness* can become just that—words!

I am reminded of Gilbert Keith Chesterton's statement that "sometimes we need to ponder the too familiar until it becomes unfamiliar to us" in order to discover some new meaning.

SOME THINGS WE HAVE HEARD ABOUT FORGIVENESS

"Forgiveness is a sign of weakness." In our world of tough competition, we are led to believe that the strong hold out while only the weak give in. Forgiveness is not a sign of weakness. It is a sign of a willingness to be vulnerable. Forgiving another may open us to the possibility of future hurts. It also opens us to the possibility of new and deeper life in that relationship.

"If someone has hurt me, they deserve my punishment. I don't forgive: I get even!" Those who wish to punish and

to get even might do well to ponder the words of an old Chinese proverb that says, "The one who pursues revenge should dig two graves."

"Love means you never have to say you are sorry." These words are destructive of relationships because they give us the unrealistic impression that hurts can always heal without using healing words. We stand always in need of forgiveness from those whom we love the most.

"Forgiving is easy to do." If we hold these words to be true, we will frequently be disappointed with ourselves. In important matters, when hurts are deep and cannot be simply "solved," we need to remember that forgiveness is a process that takes time. Even with the best of intentions, we cannot always let go of all of the past hurts in one simple decision.

"Forgiving the other is always the key issue." Life is a threefold relationship with self, others, and God. Sometimes it is difficult to realize that at the heart of the healing is forgiveness from ourselves for ourselves. Looking honestly at our ways of loving and relating may lead us to let go of our resentment of another and to accept our own limitations in the relationship.

"God will never forgive me for what I did." Such a statement bears a frightening finality. It also reflects a total misunderstanding of who God is and how God's love for each of us is unconditional no matter what our failings. God's forgiveness, like God's love, is always there for us, calling us to set out again along the human journey to some place of renewed life. When we chose less than life, we hurt ourselves, not God.

The God of Christianity, a *nevertheless* God, is always ready to lift us up again and say to us, "Yes, you failed; you hurt yourself or another. *Nevertheless*, my love is there for you. My offer of life is there for you."

"In order to forgive you must forget." A basic principle to keep in mind is that a call to forgive is not an invitation to amnesia. We do remember hurts and those who hurt us. That is no measure of our willingness to forgive. We live our lives forward and only understand them backward. It is important for us to remember the past so that we are less likely to hurt ourselves or others again and in the same way.

"Forgiveness is mine. I can do it by myself." When the hurts are of some magnitude and we struggle with whether or not we even want to forgive, the words of St. Paul are a reminder of our need for strength greater than our own.

> But now in Christ Jesus you who once were far off have become near by the blood of Christ. For he is our peace, he who made both one and broke down the dividing wall of enmity . . . (Eph 2:13-14).

I am reminded of the simple words of Dietrich von Hildebrand in his book *Fundamental Moral Attitudes* when he says, "What is revealed and shines forth in an act of real forgiveness . . . is much more important and eternal than all our cultural values."

Perhaps that is precisely why it is so important to shed some of our cultural accretions from time to time, to unlearn what we may have learned about forgiveness, so that we can learn new ways of thinking.

THE QUALITIES OF A FORGIVING PERSON

Certainly the old grandfather described at the beginning of this chapter is reflective of a gentle humanness that is sometimes born of great suffering. The words in Matthew (5:23-24) when Jesus tells us to go, even from the altar of sacrifice and prayer, to be reconciled and then to return remind us that good things happen in human hearts that decide to be involved in the process of forgiving, regardless of what it asks of them.

Forgiving persons have wrestled with the human condition, with their own strengths and limitations, until they have come to a place of peace and self acceptance.

Forgiving persons, recognizing and owning their need of forgiveness, are less likely to withhold forgiveness from others. They have a quality of self-awareness that enables them to allow others to be who they are.

Forgiving persons are open channels of new life, the new life that is often accompanied with a generous measure of pain. Having forgiven themselves, they are less resistant to either the painful or joyful entrance of new life.

Forgiving persons seek to ask for and offer forgiveness in such a way that it does not strip others of their dignity and does not diminish them as persons.

Forgiving persons are able to accept the sin-scarred and sometimes bruising forms in which human life is revealed, respecting *life* wherever it is to be found.

Like the old grandfather and like Ghandi, we are sometimes afraid. We seek to be freed from those chains of fear. And, we can be!

> Sometimes we are afraid to live by the rule of God which is forgiveness, mercy and compassion, feeling that by these we shall somehow be ended. And yet, if we could bear these three through terror's doubt, daring to return good for evil, without thought of what shall come, I cannot think we should be losers.

▼ CHRISTOPHER FRY,
A SLEEP OF PRISONERS

Tears: A Healing Presence

A man no longer what he was,
Nor yet the thing he'd planned . . .
I think you will have need of tears.

▼ EDNA ST. VINCENT
MILLAY

The words of Edna St. Vincent Millay remind me of two small incidents that I witnessed recently.

I was visiting a sick child in a local hospital. The child's mother had spent the night there because the little girl, Shannah, was both very sick and very frightened.

As I arrived Shannah began to cry, tears rolling down her little cheeks. Her mother swooped her up, surrounded her with loving arms and whispered to her, "It's okay for you to cry. Mommy loves you and will be right here with you."

Earlier in the week, I had been in a large grocery store. I am not sure what triggered the tears, but, as I passed the mother and child, I heard the mother say to the little boy, "Don't be such a crybaby. Your little brother isn't crying. He's my little man." At which point, the little boy cried even harder.

Thinking back on those two children, I feel happy for Shannah because the lessons learned in childhood are often lasting. She had an opportunity to understand that tears are a part of life.

Tears can scrub out the hurts of the heart just as nature intended them to wash out our eyes.

The little boy may come to associate tears with something that is not okay about himself. He may associate tears with shame and weakness.

There are numerous stories in the gospels about grown men and women who cried. Jesus wept over Jerusalem when he thought about the hard hearts of the people there. Judas wept when he realized the nature of his betrayal of Jesus. Peter brought himself to tears through his threefold denial of even knowing who Jesus was. Martha and Mary expressed their sadness at the death of their brother through tears.

TEARS ARE FOR ALL SEASONS

There is a universal dimension to the human act of crying. No particular aspect of life has a corner on crying. People cry for joy and for sadness. They cry in times of both loss and gain. Crying is as much for the old as for the young.

Some tears have a different meaning at different times. Infants cry because it is their way of communicating pain or need to a parent. Young children cry when they cannot fully express to a parent or teacher what it is that hurts.

Teenagers shed tears associated with the difficult process of growing up and discovering who they are and what they believe in.

Adults cry when a child is hurting, when a spouse does not understand, when a friend fails to listen carefully.

People of all ages cry when they are disappointed with themselves, when carefully laid plans do not work out as had been envisioned, when something or someone significant to their lives is lost.

AND WHEN WE CAN'T CRY . . .

We may feel a sense of deep concern in the presence of someone who says, "I hurt, but I just cannot cry. I wish I could because I think I would feel better."

Words like, "I hurt very much, but, I will not cry. I will not let the person who hurt me know how much I care," can leave us with a feeling of sadness for someone who seems not to want to be healed by being free of feelings often washed away by tears.

Sometimes people can't cry because, like the little boy in the grocery store, they associate crying with weakness, with personal inadequacy, or with any one of a number of other feelings associated with not being okay as a person.

People who can't cry have to unlearn what they were once taught and then learn again some new meaning for tears.

<u>TEARS AS OUR TEACHER</u>

Human tears freely shed at important times in life can be instrumental in helping us learn important life truths.

To hurt and to cry and learn nothing from the costly process seems like wasted suffering. Edna St. Vincent Millay says, "Count as loss those tears that turn no mill." Her words somehow associate pain with some powerful force for redemption and renewal of human life.

Tears can serve as important reminders to avoid repeating past mistakes and hurting ourselves or someone else again. Tears can serve as valuable teachers of life helping us avoid what Santayana speaks of when he says, "One who does not learn from the mistakes of the past is condemned to repeat them."

So powerful is the act of crying in portraying associations with some of life's most profound feelings, that I asked several people when they last remember crying.

A woman at a weekend retreat said, "I cry whenever I think of my twenty-four-year-old son who died of AIDS. I do not cry for him because I know he is at peace, but I cry because his father never accepted the fact that he was homosexual."

A teenage girl said, "I cry and still cry almost every

day because my best friend moved far away. I wonder if I'll ever have another friend like her."

A mother said, "I cried at my son's graduation from college. His father died several years ago and his father would have been so proud of him."

A college student said, "I cried when I saw the rioting and looting in Los Angeles after the Rodney King trial. I am worried about our country and the people in this country who hurt and feel like nobody really cares."

A father said, "I cried when I walked my daughter down the aisle at her wedding. It was like a good-bye to my little girl. But, I was very happy."

Six-year-old Tommy said, "I cried when my dog, Hansie, was run over by a car. Hansie seemed always to know how I felt, especially, if I was sad, he'd sit real close to me."

A thirty-six-year-old woman told me that she cried when her parents got divorced. She said, "I think part of the tears are for the loss of my family. It'll never be the same again. I also think I cry a lot because I wonder if it will happen in my marriage too."

Tears and the Healing of the Human Heart

These and the many other people who said to me, "I cried when . . ." reinforced my own deepest conviction that tears freely shed, tears cherished by ourselves and held sacred by someone who cares about us, are one of the most important channels for human healing and learning. They can lead us to insights into feelings sometimes tucked too carefully away.

When I read the following thoughts of Wordsworth, I wanted to add a final line . . . and so I shall.

> Thanks to the human heart by which we live,
> Thanks to its tenderness, its joys, its fears.
> To me the nearest flower that blows can give
> Thoughts that often lie too deep for tears.

But, the healing of the human spirit in sometimes small, and in sometimes dramatic ways, will happen when thoughts too deep for tears emerge at some grace-filled moment leading us beyond tears to hope and happiness.

Fear: Friend or Foe?

Fear not, for I have redeemed you;
I have called you by your name: you are mine.
When you pass through the water, I will be
   with you;
in the rivers you shall not drown. . . .
For I am the Lord, your God.

▼ ISAIAH 43:2-3

Fear is a part of every human life. We know when we are afraid. Often the feeling is inescapable in its intensity and jarring in its ability to affect us.

Sometimes we are afraid when danger lurks or when we witness some harm being done to another person.

Sometimes we can identify neither the reason for, nor the extent of, the fear that claims us at a given moment.

We think of fear as wearing distinct faces. There is the fear that protects us from ourselves or from others.

God's word tells us that "The fear of the Lord is the beginning of wisdom" (Ps 111:10). This face of fear offers a promise of greater life.

There is a face of fear that seems to paralyze us. It interferes with decision-making and with taking responsibility for the ongoing life to which we are called.

We sometimes persuade ourselves that we are not afraid, or we give ourselves reasons for following the way of fear rather than of truth.

Another face of fear is that of the seducer, somehow persuading us to hold on when greater life necessitates our letting go.

Life has been described as a series of living between two trapezes. The trapeze we are on is comfortable because it is familiar; the second trapeze calls us to grow to some new place—frightening partly because of its unfamiliarity.

Fear often enters in to give us reasons for remaining where we are. However, the only way to discover some new aspect of life is to let go and to feel the tension of being suspended between the familiar and the unfamiliar.

The face of fear that nurtures and protects us, that frees us and invites us to discover life, is like the fear that a loving parent teaches a very young child in order to save that child from harm: the fear of a hot stove, of an electric socket, of the traffic on a busy street, of a stranger.

This nurturing face of fear, important as it is, will not be the subject of reflection from this point on. Rather, the fear I wish to explore is that which can rob us of life's possibilities by subtly persuading us that security is the greatest value. The fear lurks nearby as an ever-present companion.

It was this fear that led the servant to bury the talent he had been given by a generous master and to earn for himself the harsh words of the master, "You wicked, lazy servant" (Mt 25:25).

To explore the harmful role that fear sometimes plays in life, each of us might begin by asking, "How and when has fear played an important part of either restricting my vision or limiting my life decisions? When have I failed to make a decision because I was afraid?"

The faces of this form of fear are many. They include fear of failure, fear of what others will say or think, fear of not being liked or understood, fear of God's punishment, fear of the unknown, fear of change, fear of not having all the information.

Sometimes, when we are afraid, we wish to hide our fears from others. We act as though we are filled with confidence, rather than owning the fear and dealing with it.

We are like the school teacher in *The King and I* who

sings, "Whenever I feel afraid, I hold my head erect and whistle a happy tune so no one will suspect I'm afraid."

The problem with this way of approaching fear is that, if it is practiced often enough, we may lose touch with our feelings so that we no longer recognize healthy forms of fear when they present themselves to us for our protection.

In his book *To a Dancing God*, Sam Keen engages in what he titled a "Dialogue with Fear." The dialogue reveals the personal reflection of a man whose life has been significantly influenced by fear.

Fear claims to be a valuable companion and friend who demands no change, asking only that the man not step outside the limits that fear has set.

The man in the dialogue, who is beginning to have insights into the paralyzing nature of the fear he has chosen as a companion, responds to the taunting of fear, saying,

> You demand the most alive part of me. You promise security so long as I surrender my autonomy, my critical ability, my reason, my responsibility for reflecting upon and evaluating my own experience. Your price for comfort is giving up growth. . . . Decision is the alternative to fear.

We remember the account of Adam who used fear as an excuse for avoiding God's call: "The Lord God then called to the man and asked him, 'Where are you?' He answered, 'I heard you in the garden; but I was afraid . . . so I hid myself'" (Gn 3:9-10).

God's invitations to life are many and persistent. Often such messages of life are accompanied by tension and fear as we realize that costly change is inevitable if we listen and respond to God.

When we listen carefully, we come to realize that fear is not necessarily, in and of itself, destructive. Like many other life forces, the impact of fear is determined by the response we choose to make.

If we allow fear to dominate our lives, we later regret the good left undone, kind words not spoken, friendship not shared, and risks for life not taken.

Our lives may shrivel instead of expand; our possibilities may be reduced instead of multiplied.

In the end, our lives may resemble the soul as described by Bernanos:

> Won't damnation be the tardy discovery, the discovery much too late, after death, of a soul absolutely unused, still carefully folded together, spoiled, the way precious silks are spoiled when not used.

Identifying the Life Signs by Which We Live

We live in an age when messages are forced upon us with ever greater intensity and seductiveness. We are bombarded by volumes of high-powered advertising, such that few of us can be aware of the ways in which we are influenced. We risk the possibility of losing touch with either the presence or the meaning of important life signs. Sometimes it is only in looking back that we notice we have changed.

Driving along many major thoroughfares in this country, we are often literally walled in by a myriad of billboards, each of which reflects the attempt to persuade the consumer to believe whatever the sign says about a product. I am reminded of a parody I once read of Joyce Kilmer's poem "trees":

> I think that I shall never see
> A billboard as lovely as a tree,
> And, if that billboard doesn't fall,
> I may never see a tree at all.

The element of humor does not obscure the seriousness of the challenge: retaining an awareness of our own values and of those things which motivate us to act. In a society that gives little expression to self-reflection and the importance of being inner-directed, we may find few companions along the way of the inner journey.

Meditation by Distraction: An Invitation to Recognize Life Signs

Several years ago I had the privilege of having a priest as a retreat director who announced on the first evening of our seven days together that he wanted to remove from us the impossible burden of seeking to be free of distraction during prayer. He stated that it was his purpose to help us learn to use whatever distractions we had as the framework around which to fashion our prayer during any given period of time.

I have forgotten many of his suggestions as to how this might be helpful for us as beginners. However, I remember well his description of how he trained himself to notice whatever was around him as he drove through cities—the remains of a burned building, a bridge, a factory, some street sign.

Since that time, I have made a special point of noticing highway markers and traffic signs. I began to think of these in terms of the life signs that have affected me in one way or another.

Personal Life Signs Important to Us

The bookstores are replete with volumes dealing with the impact of the family of origin. The work of those dealing with the adult children of alcoholics are reminders of the crippling effects of dysfunctional family patterns passed on, all too often unconsciously, from one generation to another. The identification of the signs by which a family lived is one of the vital steps to the possibility of full life in the present and hope for a meaningful future.

Once we have identified some of the signs by which we have lived, we can make choices that will give new meaning and direction to the present and to the future.

In my own family, we learned, even as children, the value of work. "Work hard" is a sign I still carry with me. "Do well whatever you do" was another oft-spoken message. Perhaps an unspoken part of the message was "Do better than others."

A spoken message was "Every gift you have was meant to be shared." "Leave the world a better place than you found it" was a message I heard throughout the lives of both of my parents. Inside of me a message formed that came out something like "Save the world—all by yourself, if necessary."

We can remember words we heard from our families that remain with us. Perhaps we can identify some signs that we have replaced with others of our own making as we grew up.

There is evidence that each person's past does affect both the present and the future. Dealing with a personal past may be like removing scar tissue that threatens personal prospects for a more happy and hope-filled present and future.

The following are some of the influences that come to us through a larger family—the society in which we live.

"Pain is, of itself, evil and ought to be removed as quickly as possible." This message plagues both the health care industry and the counseling services. With all of our sophisticated technology, there is still not a certain way to remove every form of physical pain instantly. Certainly, the hurts of the heart are not reducible to simple and solvable formulas.

The expectation that suffering can be removed frustrates the hurting person and obscures exploration of the meaning that suffering has in human life. Suffering has a unique power-filled way to call the hurting person to reach beyond the comfortable places of life and to reach into undiscovered possibilities.

"New is better; replaceability is a value for the '90s." The environmentalists have taken leadership in heightening our awareness that our throwaway mentality will have to be reconsidered. We are naive if we believe this throwaway mentality has not touched our approach to relationships and human values.

To walk through life with the belief that nothing lasts and that replacing is better than keeping has brought us to a crisis in the environment which is all too apparent today. It has also brought us to a casual approach to relationships that devalues the sacredness of persons and the connectedness of all life on this planet.

"There is an answer for every human question; every form of information is readily available in this computer age." This approach to life leads some of us to believe that if we can find the right guru, software, or psychiatrist, we will never have to live with uncertainty. Yet, uncertainty is inseparable from the human journey and often leads to an experience of greater wisdom. Uncertainties begin to reveal glimpses of possible, new directions.

"Power is measured by the degree of control we have over the things and persons around us." It is becoming increasingly evident to large segments of the human family that the true power in the universe lies not outside the human person in possessions and wealth, but inside the human person. It is a power that is discovered in times of prayer and self-reflection. It is the kind of power of which Jesus spoke when he said, "The kingdom is within you."

"Sexual compatibility is the best indicator of the bonds that exist between persons." The continued emphasis on the sexual dimensions of relationships is capable of destroying the tenderness and sacredness with which persons might approach one another.

The continued focusing on the sexual dimensions of relationships gives evidence of encouraging a kind of violence. Personal boundaries are violated. Human hearts are broken with the impossible burden of relationships that have only an outer appearance but lack the strength that comes from within each person.

These are but a few of the cultural signs with which we are surrounded—signs which are, in the last analysis, destructive of the sacredness of each person's life and relationships.

A brief look at some common street and road signs together with a hint at whose primary sign it may be, might prove helpful in making these reflections more practical.

YIELD	The sign of the conflict-avoider.
ONE WAY ONLY	The sign of the rigid person.
WRONG WAY	The sign of the protective person who wishes to help others avoid mistakes.
DEAD END	The sign of the cynic in describing life.
NO STOPPING/ NO STANDING	The sign of the person who is always busy.
OPEN 24 HOURS A DAY	The sign of the compulsive giver.
DANGER	The ever-present sign of the habitual risk-avoider.
WRONG WAY	The sign of the moralist.
PRIVATE/ NO TRESPASSING	The sign of the introvert.

The above is not to be taken more seriously than it deserves. It is offered with the hope that you may grow more aware of the life signs by which you live and to which you instinctively respond.

The impact of the retreat master who spoke of "meditating by distraction" remains with me as I retain some heightened awareness of the influences that surround me. Noticing life messages wherever they are to be found can be helpful in discovering the sometimes hidden keys to the life to which God calls us.

Unintended Journeys: Responding to Life's Surprises Along the Way

In his poem "The Road Not Taken," Robert Frost describes human decision-making in terms that imply choices for greater life. He says,

> Two roads diverged in a wood, and I—
> I took the one less traveled by,
> And that has made all the difference.

Earlier in the poem, he tells of how he could have chosen either way, that both had the possibility of leading to some place of new life.

But, there is another way that has the potential to call us to new life—it is a call that comes not through decision-making, but rather through some surprise event which propels us onto another course, without choice, and, as often as not, with great fear and uncertainty. I am speaking of what I choose to call the "unintended journey." These are journeys that have no advanced planning, no prior options, and no clear outcome.

I met a woman in Charleston, South Carolina, whose home and small business had been devastated by Hurricane Hugo. This woman (I shall call her Judith) told me that she had lost everything, all of it uninsured. "My life cannot ever be the same again. I must find some new place to live and some new way of making a living," she said. "Building a dream out of such ruins will not be simple."

I remember the tears in the eyes of Sandra, a woman thirty-six years of age, when she told me of a recently discovered cancer and the dreadful effects of the chemotherapy she faces each month. "This disease has changed every facet of my life. No relationship is the same. I am afraid and angry. If I live, what sort of life can I hope for?"

A high school senior, called "an all-around athlete" by his coaches, was thrown from an all-terrain vehicle and regained consciousness to discover he would never walk again. For Jeff, the options for life no longer seem as promising as they once did. For the first time in his young life, Jeff comes to terms with dimensions of his life over which he has no control.

For Judith and Sandra and Jeff, the reality of the unintended journey is all too clear. In each, there are some common denominators.

SOME CHARACTERISTICS OF THE UNINTENDED JOURNEY

Unintended journeys may be initiated by an enriching intersection of lives, by success in one's business or profession, or some other happy and unexpected turn of events. But all too often the journey of which we speak is not born of happy circumstances. Rather, it arises out of what is perceived as human tragedy or misfortune.

▼ Often there is an element of surprise. There is no way that one might have prepared for an appropriate response.

▼ On this journey, fear is a common companion. People question their ability to survive.

▼ Some high personal cost and involvement is necessary. There is neither a comfortable nor an easy way to enter into this part of the journey to greater life.

▼ Because it is often necessary to let go of something that has been very important (health, position, security), there is a sense of worry about the final outcome.

▼ Because the place in which a person journeys is unfamiliar, there is an urgent feeling of insecurity, fear of the unknown.

▼ Because the personal losses involved are substantial—however different the forms of loss—there is the process of grieving with which one must come to terms.

▼ Loneliness is a constant companion. No one else has ever made this same journey in this same way.

These and other common denominators of the unintended journey are reminders of the question that will often evolve: "Is this journey of mine a dead end or a doorway to a new life?"

The answer to this question cannot be immediately known. The answer is dependent on the choices we make. It is dependent on the support systems we seek. The answer is dependent on the faith we have in the presence of God whose love is there for us, calling us to grow far beyond the easy and familiar places of life to some place of yet undiscovered strength and hope.

Unknown to ourselves, we are often our own worst enemy. It is possible to set roadblocks along the way which turn the potential doorway into a dead end.

SOME POSSIBLE ROADBLOCKS TO LIFE

▼ Refusal to let go of what has been but no longer is represents one of the first roadblocks to new life. It is not a simple process, nor is it a single-step process. We will let go again and again. Finally, one day we let go and do not go back.

▼ Self-pity is a subtle but destructive companion for a hurting person. Perhaps only the presence of a challenging friend will lead us to identify and then reject this enemy.

▼ Our unwillingness to allow ourselves to grieve for that which we have lost interferes with progress. The starting place is some good information about the many faces of grief and the emotional signs evident in a grieving person.

▼ The absence of personal skills in dealing with the wide range of human feelings—feelings such as anger, guilt, fear, sadness, frustration—leads many people to either deny or ignore certain feelings.

The energy of these feelings may then be turned to cause greater harm.

▼ The failure to see human life for what it is, a never-ending journey with many unforeseen turns and byways, can lead us on a wild goose chase. It is necessary to see that life is a journey that God's provident love offers us a lifetime to make. Yet life is also a journey which we would like to complete early, so that we might settle in and be comfortable for the rest of our lives.

▼ Sometimes it is unhealed hurt from the past that complicates the healing of a present hurt.

THE POSSIBLE GIFTS ALONG THE WAY OF THE UNINTENDED JOURNEY

If we begin, however reluctantly, to set out on this mysterious journey, there are some rewards that emerge along the way.

▼ The gift of tears is both cleansing and humanizing. It is one of the many common bonds we share with others who are willing to open their lives to companions along the way.

▼ A greater sense of compassion is a common mark of those who have entered into their suffering. We see this compassion in the old man in the film *A Tale of Two Cities*. When asked if he would strike out against those who have harmed his, he replies simply, "In suffering, one can learn many things. To avoid bringing hurt into the lives of others is one of those lessons I have learned."

▼ Hearts that have hurt sometimes grow more aware of their own need for forgiveness and healing. Recognizing our own need for forgiveness can lead us to an understanding of why Ghandi called forgiveness "the virtue of the brave."

▼ Doubting that we may have the inner resources to survive the journey can lead to a profound understanding of the importance of sharing the journey. It is in the act of sharing that the strength we offer to another can come back into our own lives.

▼ Reflection on the gospel and the stories of Jesus can help us to identify with the unintended journeys of Jesus. We may then understand the agony that led Jesus to call out to the Father, "If it is possible, let this cup pass from me" (Mt 26:39).

▼ If we set out on the journey, however faltering our hearts and however stumbling our feet, we will recognize the truth that . . .

> like blind men and women we grope in a world of textures, afraid to touch the jagged edges of life . . . but, the one who reaches out to embrace life discovers that those same jagged edges which have pierced us have also made us strong . . . that we have grown stronger at some of those broken places.

▼ AUTHOR UNKNOWN

Gratitude:
A Life-Giving Attitude

Those of us who live in rural America have heard much about farm crises. We see pictures in the paper of auctions, which are often held against the desire of those who may have owned their farms for a very long time.

The stories read and pictures seen took on dramatic meaning recently when I spoke with a farmer and his wife. His description of the many ways in which the loss of their farm had affected his family will not soon leave my memory.

His voice was soft and controlled and his eyes were dry as he spoke of his hurts. The farmer said, "The loss of our family farm is the loss of everything for me as a man. I feel like a failure and a disappointment to many generations. To think that this farm should have been lost while I was running it. A good man provides for his wife and family. My children are grown and married. But my wife and I have almost nothing as we face the later years of our life. I wonder who I am, now that I am a farmer without a farm."

As he continued to speak, he revealed no hope for ongoing life. He seemed so near despair. I felt helpless to speak any word that might somehow lift his spirits.

In that moment, some words of St. Paul took on a new meaning for me. They were words I had sometimes questioned.

> Bear with one another; forgive whatever grievances you have against one another. Forgive as the Lord has forgiven you. Over all these virtues put on love, which binds the rest together. . . . Christ's peace must reign in your hearts. . . . Dedicate yourselves to thankfulness (Col 3:13-15).

Sometimes it had seemed to me that we are naturally and spontaneously grateful for the good things in life. At those times, gratitude seemed an effortless and always present attitude.

The wife of the farmer began to speak to him. She said, "We are good people. We have worked hard and done our best. After a marriage of twenty-eight years we have three beautiful and happy children. We have our health and, most important of all, we have each other. Clinging to the thoughts of these blessings and thanking God for them each day is what keeps me going."

Her words were an invitation to understand that gratitude is never a given. Expressing thanks is not always easy. There is a choice involved in expressing thanks. It would require effort for that farmer to remember the many things for which he could yet be grateful despite his many and pain-filled losses.

Then I remembered the words of a woman whose husband had died very recently. She told me that his death had led her near to despair and to suicidal thoughts. A good friend had suggested that every single day she should make the effort to write down one thing for which she was grateful at that moment.

She showed me her list which had an item added each day. It began with such basic things as "I can walk." "I can talk." "I have a home." "I have food to eat." And so it continued.

She described what a difficult exercise this had been for her in the beginning. She also said that she gradually experienced a change in herself as she faithfully made the effort to count her blessings.

In the familiar story of the ten lepers who were cured, we find Jesus asking a question about possible obstacles to giving thanks. "Ten were cleansed, were they not? Where are the other nine? Has none but this foreigner returned to give thanks to God?" (Lk 17:17-18)

Ten persons were healed of a powerful and much dreaded disease. How could it be that nine go away without taking time to say "thank you" to their healer? So caught up in the joy of the gift, they forgot about the giver.

SOME POSSIBLE MANIFESTATIONS OF LACK OF THANKFULNESS

Refusal/failure to discover our gifts. Each of us is created as a uniquely precious gift by a God who loves us.

It takes a lifetime and no small amount of effort and energy to discover the many gifts that are ours. Sometimes because we are afraid or simply weary of the human journey, we fear to make that inward journey that will lead us to an awareness of our many gifts.

Refusal/failure to share our gifts. My father used to tell me that every talent or gift given to us was not given for ourselves alone but was rather meant to be shared. To fail to share our gifts is a way of refusing to offer some part of us. As an old song says, "Isn't it a pity, forgetting to give back?"

Refusal/failure to affirm the gifts of others. When we do not take time or make the effort to acknowledge and affirm the gifts of others, we take something from ourselves as well as from them. Gifts affirmed grow stronger; gifts acknowledged are further set free.

Refusal/failure to believe in God's unconditional love and acceptance of us. We are created human and loved by God just as we are. Our difficulty in accepting the armful of life that is involved in being human sometimes stands between us and our acceptance of God's love for us.

Perfectionism. We are not perfect and we never can be. Only God is perfect. To expect ourselves to be perfect is to deny who we are and who we can become with God's grace. It is a failure to accept ourselves.

Preoccupation with our own pain, loss, or sense of failure. To the extent that we invest our energy in dwelling on what has been taken from us or is lost to us, we are missing the part of life that is yet gift and yet remains.

Long-term self-pity strips us of almost everything in the end.

Refusal/failure to speak the words of thanks. We can all too easily come to take for granted those persons and things for which we are filled with thanks.

Jesus tells the story of the master who gave a generous gift to each of ten servants. He then set out on his own journey. We are reminded of the ways in which gratitude can manifest itself.

The master returns and calls to the servants for an expression of their stewardship of his generous gifts. We hear words of praise for the servants who made choices about how to show their gratitude for the master's generosity. We hear harsh words as the last servant offers the excuse of wanting to safeguard the gift and of hiding it rather than investing it well. The master says to the ungrateful servant, "With your own words I shall condemn you, you wicked servant." (Lk 19:22).

These words must have come as a surprise. The servant expected the master to be pleased with his cautious response to the safeguarding of an unexpected gift.

These words are a strong reminder to us to be more aware of the many faces of ingratitude. These words are a reminder to be more willing to seek out and commit ourselves to the words of St. Paul: Dedicate yourselves to thankfulness.

Letting Go:
The Most Difficult Step
of a Long Journey

There is a singer everyone has heard
Loud, a mid-summer and mid-wood bird.

The question that he frames in all but words
Is what to make of a diminished thing.

▼ ROBERT FROST

When Robert Frost presents us with the question of what to do with a "diminished thing," he opens for our consideration many questions about failed expectations and broken dreams. He leads us into the real world of recognizing that some options are no longer available to us, though many others are.

In a way typical of a poet, Frost captures something of both the feeling and the meaning of transition times in life and in relationships. Sometimes, to continue to be fully alive in the way God wishes for us necessitates leaving some familiar place and entering into some new and, therefore, uncertain place.

The Cost of Letting Go

There is perhaps no area of human life that is more universal, or more pain-filled, for us than that of significant relationships. At times, these significant relationships can be either completely broken or dangerously weakened, and in need of being revitalized.

When we choose to enter into new relationships, it is nearly impossible for us to even give thought to the possibility of either loss or diminishment.

Searching for ways to bring new life to a friendship that is caught in the doldrums is never easy. It requires of us costly effort. It requires of us the involvement of our best and most creative energies.

Having the courage to let go of dreams that are broken and to fashion new dreams is as costly to us as was the death and resurrection of Jesus.

The courage to let go requires faithfulness to our own lives. It requires faithfulness to the ever-present call of a pursuing God who promises that in every ending are the threads of a new beginning if we but look and listen.

Jesus' Journey Sheds Light on Our Journey

The journey of Jesus from Good Friday through Pentecost is a reminder of the cost of new life and of letting go. It can serve as a source of hope for us. Jesus' death on the cross involved the loss of a life that was familiar to him, and to those who loved Him.

When we celebrate Easter, we are remembering that this was, for Jesus, the entrance into some new and unfamiliar form of life. As the risen Jesus returns and is present to some of his followers, the relationships have changed for him and for them.

The Ascension reminds us again of letting go of the old forms of life. It involves another kind of letting go for Jesus.

And then we find in Pentecost the power-filled awareness in his followers of the presence of a Jesus whose journey involves us now in the receiving of some new spirit of life.

OUR HOPES AND DREAMS CAN BRING ABOUT MUCH SELF-QUESTIONING

When dreams are lost or lose their vitality, we may ask ourselves why we did not notice that something so important to us was gradually diminishing. We ask ourselves why we did not listen to, or read more clearly, the signs that were there all along.

For us as Christians, finding power in the life of Jesus lies in our ability to identify with this human passing over from death and letting go to a new form of life, and to the celebration of a new spirit of life.

One of the painful questions at the heart of any loss of an important relationship, or the loss of the way the relationship has been, is, "What do I do now with this 'diminished thing' which was once a sacred place of vitality?"

All too often valuable energy is lost in asking the question, "Why?" or, "Why me?" This approach, as it relates to loss and letting go, will only further frustrate and weary us.

Every time we grow to some new place we leave behind some familiar place. The familiar place we leave behind us is no longer life-giving for us, whether what we leave behind is a job, a geographic location, or a relationship.

Sometimes, when a relationship is lost, valuable energy is spent reviewing what someone else did or did not do. This information is often the most apparent and readily available to us. But, it is also information which is of little value to us.

OUR PERSONAL SELF-KNOWLEDGE CAN MAKE (OR BREAK) OUR HOPES AND DREAMS

There are many indications that one cause of faltering or failed relationships is the lack of self-knowledge brought to the relationship. The ending of a relationship (or of one phase of it) can be a powerful incentive to make the lonely but rewarding journey in self-discovery.

A loving God created us with more gifts than we will ever live long enough to discover. Venturing into our own inner geography with faithfulness can only lead us to a greater awareness of how precious each of us is.

In the often foreign terrain of that inner geography, we have an opportunity to remember and reflect on our way of being a friend. There we can reflect on our ways of caring. There we can reflect on our ability to offer and share life without either demanding or wanting to determine the response of another.

When we begin from some Good Friday moment in our own lives, we can set out in the companionship of Jesus by remembering the process of loss, the willingness not to cling to what is no longer ours, and the openness to one day receive and celebrate life with renewed spirit and greater hopefulness.

Seeking hope and courage in the face of broken dreams or lost friendship can lead us to a place of greater vision. Here we see, perhaps for the first time, that a desire to control or manipulate may have been at the heart of some of our compulsive needs to give to others.

We may begin to identify some of the powerful and hidden expectations we have carried into relationships that were destructive of the bonds between ourselves and others.

LETTING GO OF WHAT WAS TO DISCOVER WHAT CAN BE

Perhaps only the eyes and the heart of the faithful Christian can, in the light of the life of Jesus, discover what to make of a "diminished thing." Perhaps only the one who has reflected on the ways in which death was the doorway to new life for Jesus will have the courage to look in the ruins for signs of greater life.

Recently, a friend of mine told me about a sign that hangs in her office. She said that the words are a reminder to her to continue to commit herself to discover those hidden treasures that abound in every human heart simply by reason of our creation by a loving God.

My friend said, "When I hurt, I can ask, 'Why me?' I would like to become a person who asks, 'Why not me?'"

My friend's sign says simply: "Pain is inevitable; new life is optional."

Each of us can be more care-filled and respectful of our lives

▼ by accepting whatever suffering comes into our lives,

▼ by letting go of what is no longer available to us, and

▼ by choosing faithfulness to the new life offered to us by a loving God.

Like Jesus, we can experience the truth that from death and diminishment can come renewed and radiant life.

For us, as for Jesus, the journey begins with letting go.

The Sounds of Silence

There is an appointed time for everything,
and a time for every affair under the heavens....
a time to be silent, and a time to speak.

▼ ECCLESIASTES 3:1, 7

Indeed, there is an appropriate time for both silence and speech. But time for silence seems less available to most of us.

We live in a time when technology has developed ways to magnify sound beyond volumes once imagined. Vibrations from powerful car stereo systems are capable of blasting windows out of passing vehicles. Jet airplanes fly over homes, rocking the earth and the foundations on which these homes stand. Television sets in homes are turned on early each day, and rest for only a few hours late in the night.

I recall seeking silence along the banks of the Charles River in Boston. I discovered that my walk required a continual jockeying for space with the bicyclists, skate boarders, joggers, and dogs, and it was then that I noticed that even lovers walking hand in hand were wearing headphones.

We do, indeed, live in an age of noise and hype. We live in a world where the ability of technology to reproduce and magnify sound makes it increasingly difficult to find an environment that fosters the quest for solitude and the hope of some healing sounds of silence.

WORDS THAT DISAPPEAR

An internationally renowned lexicographer was interviewed on television. He had just completed the revision of a thesaurus, and he listed and spoke about new words that were added in his revision. He also spoke about thousands of words that were removed because they no longer had meaning or relevance to our culture.

As he spoke, I wondered if *silence* might one day be such a word—a word that no longer had meaning or relevance for people whose lives are nearly overwhelmed by sound.

The words of Ecclesiastes are like a call to accountability, to each of us, to value both silence and speech. The words are an invitation to reflect on the sounds of silence that are a part of life, even as we search for the meaning of words.

The Harsh Sounds of Silence

There are sounds of silence that are not life-giving; instead, some forms of silence may limit or lessen life's possibilities.

Such is the silence that seeks to control, by refusing to talk when speech may be vital to the growth of a friendship.

Such is the silence that gives messages of rejection, by refusing to reveal one's own vulnerability.

Such is the silence that can sometimes frighten one who approaches.

So powerful is the moment in which a word is desperately needed that without it neither person can know who and where they are in relationship to one another.

A young widow recently told me of the tragic death of her husband of nine years. I was saddened when she recounted the story of what she called a "troubled marriage," a marriage which, she said, would have ended in divorce had her husband not died.

She said, "We gradually stopped talking to one another because we were afraid and because we lacked the skills needed to listen to one another's feelings."

The harshness of a silence that is not broken becomes as destructive as it is pain-filled.

What the young woman described, in her sadness

and regret, was spoken by Robert Frost in his poem "Revelation":

> We make ourselves a place apart
> Behind words that tease and flout
> But, oh, the agitated heart
> Till someone really finds us out . . .
> So all who hide too well away
> Must speak and tell us where they are.

It is important that we learn to identify and share our feelings, naming them gently for a friend whose companionship is important to us. But, primarily, it is naming and owning them for our friendship with ourselves that is important.

Each time a feeling is hidden away, each time that we remain silent, when speaking would leave us more vulnerable and stronger inside ourselves, we hurt ourselves and others.

The words of Phyllis McGinley cannot be ignored:

> Sticks and stone may break my bones,
> aimed with angry art.
> Words can sting like anything
> But silence breaks the heart.

Such harsh sounds of silence can, and do, break both hearts and friendships.

THE GENTLE SOUNDS OF SILENCE

There is a time to speak and a time to be silent, for each can lead us to the inward journey of the heart. Each can be an important component of prayer and self-reflection, without which no life can grow more human and more loving.

We are put on this earth for one purpose only and that purpose is to learn to love. Both speech and silence are a part of that learning process.

There is a silence that communicates love just as deeply as do the precious words, "I love you." It is the silence of friends, comfortable in each other's presence and no longer needing to fill each moment with words. It is the silence of a parent, simply holding a young child, that communicates through the gentle and silent language of touch.

Inner silence can be experienced when time is spent in a favorite place—beside the ocean . . . on a mountainside, where one can look for miles into the silent valleys . . . at a graveside, where parents, whose death is remembered there, communicate through some silent language.

There also is the inner silence that one can experience simply by turning off all television sets, radios, and CD players and sitting in the quiet of one's home.

There is the choice of a stance toward life that seeks to listen carefully to where we have already been so that we can better choose the direction we want for both the present and the future.

There is a stance toward life that seeks to listen, helps heal past hurts, and ensures against repeating past mistakes.

Jesus spoke of people who had ears but could not hear and eyes but would not see.

In a world filled with so many demanding external sounds, the challenge of choosing a time for silence, for prayer and self-reflection, may be as complicated as it is redeeming.

Intimacy:
A Challenge and a Need

Eloquent essays have been written about the power of human words. Robert MacNeil offered his ideas in a book titled Wordstruck. We are sometimes cautioned about the ways in which we use words and the impact, for good or for ill, that we may have on others through the words we speak and the manner in which we speak them.

Words can have a kind of ambiguity so that a single word may evoke very different images in different people. One such word is *intimacy*. Its most profound meaning and its creative possibility can best be realized when we strip away fabrications and misconceptions about the nature and the price of intimacy.

I asked several people of varying ages and from different lifestyles what came to their minds when I said the word *intimacy*. The following are some of the responses.

A forty-three-year-old married woman said, "Sharing of a lifetime . . . Trusting and respecting . . . Being two separate persons . . . It is not just sex, nor is it primarily sex."

A twenty-six-year-old male waiter, not married, said, "Sex." And then after a brief pause, he added, "But, more than that, too. Like sharing what you cannot often share . . . Talking about what really matters . . . Feeling a good friend near."

An unmarried thirty-five-year-old woman who called herself an artist and a poet said, "I take the stuff of intimacy seriously . . . It is context, texture, flavor, sound, sensation for life . . . We can experience it in many ways . . . Listening . . . Just being present to . . . Being mutually vulnerable and mutually respectful. . . ."

A twenty-five-year-old aspiring male actor said, "It is created by sharing our stories . . . I cannot be intimate unless I can tell the other person that I am sometimes afraid and feel vulnerable . . . It is telling the truth even when that is difficult . . . Sex would be about twentieth on my list."

As I began to reflect on what I had heard, I began to formulate my own understanding of what it means to share intimacy with another person. I was also keenly aware of how essential intimacy is to our quest for the full human life to which Jesus invited us when he said, "I came so that they might have *life*" (Jn 10:10). I look upon intimacy as a process rather than a product. With effort and commitment we can develop the skills and do the difficult work deep inside our souls that can make intimacy possible.

My reflections on intimacy focus on the words in Ezekiel 36:26-27:

> I will give you a new heart and place a new spirit within you, taking from your bodies your stony hearts and giving you natural hearts. I will put my spirit within you.

The desire to grow toward human intimacy can be thought of as a process of transforming a human heart from stone to flesh. There are some characteristics common to hearts in need of transformation. These include:

▼ Hearts that place a higher value on being perfect rather than growing through and in the human condition.

▼ Hearts that lack flexibility and therefore are resistant to growing and changing as an expected part of life.

▼ Hearts that judge others harshly and without allowance for the unexpected circumstances every person faces.

▼ Hearts that seek to control their own lives and those of others with no facility for letting go and moving on when that is what life demands.

▼ Hearts that are too insecure to allow themselves to be vulnerable and will not risk the possibility of being hurt.

▼ Hearts that have no place for laughter and play and cannot tolerate life's inconsistencies.

The quest for intimacy, the process of growing in our ability to enter into the lives of others and to allow them in at more than a surface level, will involve us in a multi-faceted journey where we approach life with open minds and hearts. We will necessarily come to recognize that it is a journey involving, at a most fundamental level, our relationship to self, our ability to cherish and take possession of self in such a way that we need not compromise who we are nor do we need to give ourselves away to relate to another at more than a superficial level.

Though intimacy is better experienced than defined, like *home* we know when we have it and when we are there. Intimacy derives some of its beauty, value, and preciousness from the very fact that it is necessarily a somewhat limited commodity neither easily nor quickly attained.

Both separation and connection are essential to the process of intimacy. Sometimes it is in the spaces that exist between ourselves and a friend that we discover new growing edges for greater meaning and depth. Sometimes we find the vibrancy in sacred moments shared without need of words.

Dietrich Bonhoeffer says that "nothing can fill the gap when we are away from those we love, and it would be wrong to try and find anything. . . . [L]eaving the gap unfilled preserves the bonds between us."

The two great commands to love God and our neighbor as we love ourselves are a constant reminder that we can neither live nor grow in isolation. The challenging aspect of our need for intimacy is that we are not adequately nourished by having only superficial interactions with others. Trying to live without the risks of being intimately involved with at least a few good friends is to risk a kind of spiritual malnutrition. It is in the meaningful overlapping of human lives that our souls can more readily unfold and expand into new and wider horizons.

The cultural milieu in which we find ourselves at this point in time does not foster or even seem to understand the nature of prayerful solitude, without which we lack the ability to identify our own personal boundaries and run the risk of invading the sacred space of others.

Author Virginia Satir names some key aspects of the groundwork on which intimacy can exist when she speaks of loving without clutching, joining without invading, and inviting without demanding.

The journey in intimacy may well begin with identifying the places and ways in which our hearts are stony, unwelcoming, and fear-dominated. God's promise to replace our hearts of stone demands that we be involved in fulfilling that promise. That means staying alive and awake, noticing when we are absent even from ourselves and, therefore, incapable of offering a loving presence to another.

When we are open to and invested in the transformation of our hearts of stone, we will recognize in ourselves an added degree of the acceptance of others just as they are because we are more respectful and loving toward our own limitations and gifts. We will be more free to risk and less afraid of failure. Because we have been involved in an inward journey, we will be more familiar with the inner geography of our own hearts. Then we can offer the words of the poet e. e. cummings with some insight into their meaning:

> i carry your heart with me (i carry it in my heart) i am never without it (anywhere i go you go . . .)

> i carry your heart (i carry it in my heart)

Room Enough for Pain

Man has places in his heart which do not yet exist, and into them enters suffering in order that they may have existence.

▼ LEON BLOY

One of the difficulties we sometimes have with God's word is our propensity to hear the words as if they are some form of truth which can be fitted neatly into a place that is at once comfortable and reassuring.

I am reminded of the face of a five-year-old girl named Tammy who was a member of our children's group at the local shelter for battered women.

One particular afternoon we were going to read a story about pain. We asked the children to think of a time in the past few days when they had felt hurt or been sad, and to tell us what had happened to trigger the feelings.

As we continued around the circle, it became little Tammy's turn to speak. She said, "My name is Tammy, and I could have felt sad two days ago, but, you see, I have this little switch in my head. . . ."

As she said the words, she held her little hand in front of her face as if to demonstrate her words as she continued on, "And, when I could feel sad, I just turn my little switch and all the hurt goes away."

SHUTTING OFF OUR FEELINGS LIMITS OUR LIVES

I wondered how many times in the last few days Tammy had "turned her little switch" in order to survive the hurt she was feeling.

I wondered how long it might be, if she continues to rely on that switch, before she would no longer know what she was feeling.

I wondered if little Tammy would come to have the lifeless eyes I have sometimes seen in other children at the shelter. These other children are no longer willing or able to name their feelings. It hurts too much to identify them and then share their feelings with someone who cares.

To live and grow as human beings involves experiencing and dealing with a wide range of feelings— some of which are happy and hope-filled, some of which are sad and pain-ridden.

There is no transformation process possible for the person who seeks to set a selective filter, which will allow some feelings to enter into life while blocking others.

Joseph Needleman in his book *The Way of the Physician* says that human beings cannot grow more conscious of important truths while remaining continually comfortable.

ADULTS TOO CAN HAVE THEIR "LITTLE SWITCHES"

My concern for little Tammy and the frequency with which she uses her "little switch" has to do with her setting patterns of denial, whose destructiveness is directly related to how often she hurts too much to feel her pain.

Every one of us has feelings that we either deny or have denied, for various periods of time and for different reasons.

Some of us deny that we are angry, frustrated, intimidated, frightened, or even happy at any given moment because of some instinct in us that tells us that any one of these feelings will not be acceptable to someone else.

Some of us deny certain feelings because we learned that some feelings are either naughty or unacceptable to God, our parents, or a teacher.

We have our own grown-up form of "little switches" which we adjust that can be just as destructive for us, if used too often, as Tammy's may be to her.

One of the reasons for the group to which Tammy belongs is to offer her an environment where her feelings are listened to and cared about, where she is cared about in such a way that she will not need to shut out her hurt and sadness.

Facilitators of the group give suggestions about appropriate and inappropriate ways to deal with feelings so that the children come to believe that their feelings are sacred and can unlock some doors to a happier life for each of them.

THE GOSPEL WEAVES TOGETHER PAIN, LIFE, AND TRUTH

Tammy, like the rest of us, lives in a society where the common messages about pain, in any form, are: Run away from it. Get rid of it immediately. Deny it. Avoid it. View it as evil. Look upon it as necessarily and always destructive.

Often we forget, or we do not take seriously, the messages of the gospel and the example of the life of Jesus, in which human suffering is identified as a part of every human life, not as punishment from God for sin committed.

When we seek to live very closely to the values given to us by Jesus, life may often have added moments of pain and discomfort. We will often be out of step with others who do not share the vision of Christianity.

Human life is not a spectator sport where we can sit on the sidelines, safe and secure, while others fight the battle on the field. Life is, by its very nature, self-involving and potentially painful as well as joyful.

Sometimes we just go along with our lives, much like sleep-walkers who, at any given moment, may not feel hurt simply because we are not fully aware.

And sometimes, it is only at the moment of some

tragedy that we are awakened to aspects of life that we simply had not noticed for a long time.

Tragedy and suffering are like an awakening call inviting us to be more aware of where we are going and who we are becoming. We may not like the hurt, but it can open new doors for us.

ROOM ENOUGH FOR PAIN

Several years ago I read a book by Jean Vanier called *Room Enough for Joy*. Now, in retrospect, I would like to add a second volume to the series.

It would be a book that begins with the words of Leon Bloy,

> . . . into them [those places in the heart] enters suffering in order that they may have existence.

The underlying thesis of the book would be the simple truth that human life cannot be transformed in any important and lasting way unless and until, in the heart open to receive its gifts, there is . . . room enough for pain!

Death:
The Thief in the Night,
The Bearer of Gifts

I shall die, but that is all that I shall do for death.

. . . I am not on his pay-roll.

I will not tell him the whereabouts of my friends, nor of my enemies.

Though he promise me much, I will not map him the route to any man's door.

▼ EDNA ST. VINCENT
MILLAY

It is the gift of the poet, the playwright, the artist that they can often sketch for us, in words, in color, that which is too close to us to be given expression. Words fail and images lack clarity. We are left to rely on those who can envision what we cannot.

Such is the reality of death. Dylan Thomas tells us not to "go gentle into that good night. . . . Rage, rage against the dying of the light." John Donne challenges the meaning of death with the words, "Death be not proud, though some have called thee mighty and dreadful."

Few would deny that death seems to have the last word on some aspects of the human condition. For some it is looked upon simply as an end—to life, to love, to meaning. For others, it is a rich and new beginning for greater life, for more profound love, and for deeper meaning. For all, there is an uncertain and unknown quality about death that sometimes evokes fear and sadness at the feelings of finality. Someone who once had a part in our lives is no longer available to us in familiar ways. Seeing, touching, and listening are forced into some unexplored realm that seems less satisfying than looking at, hugging, and directly hearing the voice of someone we care about.

Death has been described as a thief that comes in the night, robbing us of the presence of one who is a part of us. One could scarcely argue with such a description of something that reaches far beyond the surface of life to invade space that may have seemed inviolable. Death spoken of as an idea is vastly different from the death of one whose presence is woven into the fabric of our existence. Countless are the many valuable facets of our lives that feel stolen when someone we love dies.

But, if death is a thief, it is also, in countless ways, a

gift-giver. When family and friends come together at the time of a death the gifts are many and varied. It is important to make note of them. They include:

The gift of *presence*. Loved ones gather to care for one another, to express that care, and to offer support in the days that lie ahead. Closest friends and more casual acquaintances draw strength from one another as they gather to, as we say, "pay their respects," not only to the one who has died, but, more important, to each other. And, in this process, each receives something that will bring renewed strength.

The gift of *remembering*. When family and friends gather at the time of a death, the inevitable storytelling begins. In the sharing of events once forgotten, or of little import, many more lives are touched, and the stories seem more important. In this process, loved ones discover new meaning in their own lives.

The gift of *listening*. When a person is remembered and stories are told, those present have an opportunity to listen not only to the stories being told, but to the pain that may be underlying the need to share that event with others. Listening carefully is an expression of concern for feelings that need to be poured out. And, in this process, others present feel cared about and secure enough to reveal what is in their hearts.

The gift of *healing*. Every human life has some unhealed hurts. Every life has some precious and vulnerable places in the heart that need to be shared with others and to receive from others some words of tenderness and understanding. At the time of a death, long-standing differences and misunderstandings have the possibility of being resolved or of being opened up for future resolution. And, in this process, each person present is invited into a new place of safety and comfort.

The gift of *challenging our ways of loving*. When someone we love is taken from us, we often begin to examine how we may or may not have shown our love to that person. We may also question how we are treating those with whom we share life most deeply—spouses, children, siblings, friends. If we admit to some regrets in any of these areas, we may deepen our resolve to change and to speak our love more warmly and clearly. Sometimes people make a promise to do this in the name of the one who has died. And, in this process, each person is richer because of the life of the one who has gone before, the one in whose name family and friends have come together.

The gift of *celebration*. At the time of death, though there is mourning, a sense of loss, feelings of profound sadness and loneliness because of the vacuum with which we are left, at some point, the humorous incidents, the funny stories, the playful memories are almost certain to emerge. People begin to talk about the happy times and how this person would want to be remembered, how this person would want life to go on for those left behind. Some of the most meaningful funerals I have attended have ended with what can only be called a party in honor of the person who would have wanted it that way, and may even have let that be known to the family before the time of death. In this process of sharing in a celebration of love and laughter, the sadness and pain are not gone, but they do not seem to have the final word.

As we speak of death as a thief and a gift-giver, what can we say from the point of view of those who have died? That their lives now continue in a place where anguish and tears have no role? Shall we say that they are now in a better place from which they can continue to share life with us and cherish us? Shall we say that they are now free from some tormenting pain and no longer vulnerable to whatever it was that may have been difficult for them when they were with us here? Shall we say that they are now reunited with someone who has gone before—perhaps a spouse, a child, dear friends? And, if we say any of these things, have we not spoken of death as a giver of gifts?

When my mother died, anguished though I felt, feeling like an orphan even at my age, I had images of Daddy there, waiting to meet her. I also know that she waited many years for this reuniting because she spoke of it often.

When a cherished aunt died, I knew that my uncle was waiting for her, longing for her, waiting to make a huge party of whatever sort happens when people are no longer separated.

The following description of death might serve as a source of consolation for each of us as we say our forced good-bye at the time of death:

I am standing on the seashore. A ship at my side spreads her white sails to the morning breeze and starts for the blue ocean. She is an object of beauty and strength. I stand and watch her until at length she hangs like a speck of white cloud just where the sea and sky come to mingle with each other.

Then someone at my side says, "There, she is gone."

"Gone where?"

Gone from my sight. That is all. She is just as large in mast and hull and spar as she was when she left my side and she is just as able to bear her load of living freight to her destined port.

Her diminished size is in me, not in her. And just at that moment when someone at my side says, "There, she is gone!" there are other eyes watching her coming, and other voices ready to take up the glad shout: "Here she comes."

And that is dying.

▼ ANONYMOUS

Unlearning: A First Step to Renewed Life

"You are not as pretty as your sister."

"You failed."

"You are not a good boy."

When children listen to comments like these, they not only take them to heart, but they may also change their meaning.

"You are not as pretty as your sister" becomes "You are neither pretty nor attractive. People who aren't pretty or attractive aren't lovable."

"You failed" changes to "You are a failure. You'll probably never succeed at anything you do."

"You are not a good boy" is registered as "Shame on you. You are not a good person. It's not what you did that was bad, but you are a bad boy."

One of the problems with the statements as they are offered by the speaker, and as they are understood by the hearer, is that the sender may never know the final form of the message received.

The above and similar messages, if repeated often enough and by different persons, begin to shape a person's sense of self. And, unless something happens to unlock the box that stores these destructive words, they can affect the way a person enters into relationships with others. After all, we relate to others primarily out of our perceptions of ourselves.

UNLEARNING PRECEDES LEARNING

I recently heard a speaker on a morning talk show say, "The illiterate of today is not the person who cannot read or write. Today's illiterate is the person who cannot learn, unlearn, and learn again." I believe we might paraphrase that statement by saying,

> Any child or adult who has repeatedly received negative messages about self from significant others will find relationships very difficult, unless someone who cares assists in the process of unlearning.

> The process involves replacing the negative message with positive ones like being lovable and capable and good.

Learning to love ourselves is one of the most difficult tasks in life. It is not likely that we can be successful without the presence of loving companions who accept our faults and offer strong affirmation of our positive qualities.

Learning to love ourselves is a lifelong process of unlearning negative messages that have influenced our sense of self. What we must unlearn are really untruths that even we may have been instrumental in magnifying beyond the intent of the original speaker of the words.

HALF-TRUTHS

Besides the untruths to be unlearned, there is also a long list of what I think of as "half-truths" that have played an all too important role in our lives and in our relationships. These, too, must be unlearned in their original form and changed to enlarge their meaning.

When we think about our relationships with ourselves, we may discover that these half-truths have caused us to set aside either our pursuit of self-knowledge or our sense of self-worth.

Few of us have either understood or believed the statement of Teilhard de Chardin when he says simply, "Every human being is an irreplaceably precious gift."

When I think of half-truths that will eventually play a destructive role in relationships, each of them is related to reinforcing a poor self-image. To learn to love ourselves as "irreplaceably precious gifts," we might examine some of the adages with which many of us grew up:

It is better to give than to receive. How often have we heard and acted upon this statement. The problem is that we have failed to acknowledge that the giver is in the position of power. If we need to be the givers then we need to recognize that we are then also the ones who are in control.

A simple reflection on the difficulty each of us has in giving to a "giver friend" can help us understand why it is important to free ourselves of the above adage and to replace it with *to be a loving friend, I must learn to give and receive with equal ease.*

Selfless love is the only generous love. In relationships that are healthy, two people reach out to offer the gifts that each has and to accept the gifts offered by the other. Self does and must enter into every relationship. All that each of us has to offer to another human being is ourselves, just as we are.

All love is self-involving. No relationship that is life-giving can bear the burden of one selfless self and continue to grow in mutuality.

Always forget yourself and put others first. There certainly are times when we can and do respond to the needs of others and do put aside our own needs. We do this when someone we love loses a parent or a child to death. We do this when someone we care about loses a job or is diagnosed as having terminal cancer. We do this when a friend calls and simply needs us to listen and care.

But, there is a difference between forgetting self and putting another first when the occasion clearly demands that of us as a loving response and when forgetting self becomes the underlying rule of life for us.

Lifelong habits of always forgetting self can produce people who no longer know how to cherish and share their own needs, people who have lost the conviction, "I am an irreplaceably precious gift" with gifts and needs.

Altruistic love is the most authentic love. I do not believe that altruistic love exists. People who claim to offer altruistic love may become either exploiting or controlling without realizing it. When we seek a relationship with another person, there is always some reward in it for us.

No matter who is the recipient of either our giving or our gifts, we do not offer those gifts without having something come back to us. That is the nature of giving when it is done in a way that is respectful of the receiver.

I often think of a statement my father (who had been a lifelong teacher) once made. He said, "I teach because I enjoy it, and I realize that each year I receive and learn much more than I could ever give or teach."

Through prayer and self-reflection, we may discover some of the long hidden untruths or half-truths that we learned along the way.

AGAIN . . . AND AGAIN . . . AND AGAIN

Through prayer and self-reflection, we can become open to the difficult and sometimes pain-filled process of unlearning that prepares the way for learning again . . . and again . . . and again.

Sometimes, also, through some tragedy, some unforeseen life experience, we are challenged to examine the powerful forces at work in our lives.

Sometimes, necessity pushes us where virtue never led us, and we find ourselves examining lifelong patterns we may have long ignored.

And, we begin the process of unlearning that prepares us for learning again . . . and again . . . and again.

First Grade, First Grade: Choices We Refuse to Make

A few years ago I was invited by an eight-year-old friend named Hennessy to attend a variety show at her neighborhood elementary school. I have forgotten most of the young but poised performers who made their way onto the stage that evening. I doubt that I will ever forget the final first-grade performer, six-year-old Kayla.

Dressed in black tights and a red spangled jacket with top hat to match, she took her place on the stage. With well-placed movements, she set her black cane in position and waited for her accompanist to begin.

Her carefully crafted song was a parody of one of Sinatra's favorites, "New York, New York." Her lyrics were a recitation of the many things important to her: "I've learned my ABC's, I've learned to read . . . First Grade, First Grade . . . I've learned to share, I've learned to care . . . First Grade, First Grade." And then, she came to the final lines, and, with an appropriate measure of both class and drama, she made her point: "If you can make it there, you'll make it anywhere . . . First Grade, First Grade."

Singing like a seasoned performer, her thesis seemed undeniable. But, upon appropriate reflection, I knew that little Kayla will learn that, wonderful as it was, she simply cannot stay in first grade for the rest of her life. For at least eleven more years, there will be other grades one after another and never-ending transitions beyond that for all of her life.

One of the great mysteries in our lives as human beings is that the vast majority of us, whether out of fear, insecurity, or lack of energy, have a settler mentality that wants to stay where we are. Whether because we are very happy or because we are too intimidated by the unknown that lies ahead, we resist letting go and moving.

Sometimes I think of my own life as being like the mountains I used to climb while backpacking. Because we could see only a certain part of the climb ahead, we'd reach plateau after plateau, each time believing that the next one would certainly find us at the summit, only to discover that there was yet another height and another.

Sometimes the challenging changes of life are like climbing the mountain: they require external change of us—moving, a new job, a new city. But, not less important, and often more perplexing, are the changes continually going on in our inner geography. The ongoing process of self-discovery, coupled with our need to continually improve our ways of relating to others, can be as rewarding as it sometimes is upsetting. We are jarred loose, often out of feelings of discomfort that force us to move along to some yet undiscovered and somewhat threatening place.

One thing about life is certain: it will move along with us present to ourselves or absent from self-involvement. The change is the certain dimension. Our response is the undetermined factor in the equation of life.

Hearing little Kayla's rendition of "First Grade, First Grade" brought to mind a powerful film called *The Tin Drum*.

The story is set in Nazi Germany. A group of well-educated and financially-able adults gather to celebrate the third birthday of the son of the hosts. His most treasured present is a tin drum.

When he is sent off to bed, he crouches in the darkness at the top of the stairs, listening to his parents and their friends discussing the frightening times in which they live. Their uncertain future is plaguing them. So great is the impact of their words, so frightening are its implications, that the little boy makes a decision and resolves to avoid their plight. He says to himself, "I know what I will do, I will stay three." And, as the story unfolds, that is emotionally what he does. Whenever the pressures are too great for him, he pounds furiously on his tin drum.

Probably every human life, though in less decisive ways, bears some marks of ways in which we choose to "stay three," believing that we can then avoid some facet of our life. Eventually we will face the truth that we cannot do that and remain on the path toward life.

Staying three or choosing to stay in first grade is what we do when:

▼ we care more about what other people will say we are than what we believe we are.

▼ we do not reach out in love for fear of being rejected.

▼ we shut another door of possibility because we are unwilling to risk opening it a bit.

▼ we prefer certainty to possible life.

▼ we seek a tension-free life rather than a life-giving one.

▼ we choose not to tell the truth in a relationship for fear of harming it.

▼ we continually look at the dark side and ignore the hints of light and life.

▼ we take life too seriously and do not take time for laughter.

▼ we cling to our anger rather than acknowledging it and seeking some appropriate form of expression.

▼ we refuse to forgive because we do not want to be hurt again.

▼ we believe that being perfect is what God demands of us rather than accepting the humanness in which we are created.

▼ we refuse to forgive ourselves because to do so would be an admission of our limitations and sinfulness.

▼ we judge others harshly and cannot allow them the time and space they need to become themselves.

In these and countless other ways, we can become our own worst enemies, people incapable of accepting the lifetime that God gives to each of us to learn to love him and one another. "Life to the full" is our God-given destiny. Staying alive and awake along the way is our responsibility.

Like Peter Pan, we may say to ourselves, "I don't want to grow up," especially when we are afraid that we are not up to bearing life's hurts and realities. We fear that the whole project may become unmanageable if we go with it, relax into it, and stay on the path. All our theoretical knowledge, truisms, and axioms about growth as related to change often do not seem enough to carry us through when the moment to act on what we know arrives.

Faithfulness to life demands that we are committed to participating in life rather than in cutting it off or blocking it out. Faithfulness to life is what I believe Jung was talking about when he said that "there is no event in history comparable to the unfolding of one human life."

W. H. Auden expressed the same truth in another way in his poem "Love By Ambition":

For no is not love, no is no,
the shutting of a door
The tightening jaw
A conscious sorrow,
And saying yes
Turns love into success.

A Common Decision: To Live With Risk or Regret

My world cannot exist
behind closed doors, drawn shades
and tightly-shut eyes
wishing for that which is dead.
Close the heavy oaken door
on life, if you will
while I remain outside
open to life, nature and others
with whom we are one.
I cannot live in the past
that never existed
or in the present too intangible to grasp
but only in a future of hope
where I live without regret
knowing that I was willing to risk all.

▼ LORRAINE DRURY JACKSON

There is a certain kind of person who is dedicated to being, to doing, to loving, to giving, to seeking, to sharing, to experiencing all of life. Such a person is committed to avoiding ever having to say, "If only I had . . . ."

There is another kind of person, not an uncommon type, who is caught in the "should I?" or "should I not?" dilemma. Such a person loses tremendous amounts of energy, refusing to decide, for fear of making a mistake, for fear of what someone else will think, for fear of being rejected by reaching to another. Such a person is almost certain to be left with volumes of regret while asking the question, "Why didn't I . . . ?"

In searching for the meaning of the words *risk* and *regret*, I was surprised to discover that all of the definitions for risk carried overtones of hurt, injury, damage, loss, danger, and hazard. The life-giving faces of risk were not listed in the dictionary.

I had expected that some of the description, like that given for the word *crisis*, would include suggestions like "turning point," "for better or for worse," "a calculated decision that could result in either good or harm."

I was then reminded of words I had heard years earlier. They were the words of a wise and experienced professor from the University of Minnesota named John Brantner.

At a lecture he was delivering as a part of a series on "Death and Dying," John Brantner began his presentation in a somewhat surprising manner. He said, "I have not come here this evening to talk to you about death, but rather, about life. After a death there are some limitations on what we can and cannot do. But, during life the possibilities exist. It is up to us to choose them."

He went on to explain that the most important thing to avoid was a sense of regret, of words not offered, love not spoken, admiration never acknowledged.

He was very practical in suggesting that if there was someone we cared about who did not know that, a call should be made or a letter written. If some writer or teacher had influenced our lives in a significant way he insisted on the importance of communicating with them to let them know. His list was very long and highly specific in its purpose of avoiding feelings of regret in whatever way. He said, "Call, write, visit. . . . Say the words now. If you do this and begin to make this a way of life, you will not likely be plagued with something not easily healed—*regret*."

When John Brantner began to describe the process of grieving, he spent most of his time talking about his thesis that grief, from whatever form of loss, is facilitated by the absence of regret.

It is not uncommon for some family member to say, at the time of a funeral, "His son never knew how much his father loved him and now it is too late," or, "I believe my mother loved me but she never told me that she did."

In the film *Always*, Pete, a fire-fighting pilot, dies and is permitted time to return to observe those with whom he worked and those important to him. He reviews his friendships and his love for the woman central to his life. He either could not or would not tell this woman how important she was to him. The words "I love you" were never said to her. When he is about to leave her for the final time he says of life after death, "The love we hold back is the only pain that follows us there."

It is "risky business" to say our love, to tell a friend how much his or her presence means, to let a neighbor know how much we rely on his or her support and affirmation.

All of life is involved in taking risks. But, to risk is not an invitation to some form of folly, some careless choice that gives no thought to either personal responsibility or to consequences for ourselves and others.

The form of risk of which we speak involves weighing options, seeking information, scrutinizing implications, caring deeply about the ways in which not only our lives but the lives of others may be affected. But, having done this, we must decide.

Conscious choice-making and risk-taking involves us in self-reflection and prayer. It leads us to review past choices we may have made that are related to present ones being considered. It is an invitation to look at the ways in which we offer or withhold love for reasons of either fear or insecurity which would seem to ensure against mistakes or failure, sin or selfishness. In *The Clowns of God*, the pope in exile says to his friend, "The real sin is to be niggardly in love. To give too much is a fault easily forgiven." Cardinal Newman put it another way when he said, "I would not give much for that love which is never extravagant, which always observes proprieties."

There is something a bit dangerous about the nature of life as it unfolds because we are continually being led into another unknown place toward some decision that fails to reveal to us all that we might like to know. As we continue to grow and try to "grow up," we may begin to experience the strength that we gain when we refuse to hide from the truth of who we are, when we refuse to have fear as a major motivating force and are therefore less likely to live below the level of our best. We may avoid the unhealed sense related to regret that goes far beyond sadness and is much more difficult to erase.

In the book *Inner Simplicity*, Elaine St. James says, "Few things will liberate you faster and move you more quickly along your inner paths than doing the things you fear."

When we are motivated by fear, however well concealed it may be even from ourselves, we are in the dual realm of risk and regret. In this place there is no simple way of avoidance: It is risky to care and not to care, to love and not to love, to be open and to remain closed, to be vulnerable and to hide in "perfect strength."

To live in a world that offers the illusion of being risk-free is to live in a world where dreams can be neither fashioned nor pursued. On the other hand, to be open to the world where responsible risk-taking is seen as a part of our lives, and where there are sometimes painful consequences of risking for life, is to be open to the full human life to which we are called. In a very real sense, we do not have a choice not to risk if and when we choose to *live*.

> To be happy, and forever,
> You must see your wish come true,
> Don't be careful, don't be clever,
> When you see your wish, pursue.
> It's a dangerous endeavor,
> But the only thing to do.

▼ INTO THE WOODS

The Storyteller: A Shaper of Life

The role of the storyteller has been heightened and popularized in recent years. We have come to value the self-help group primarily as a place where people share their stories openly and without fear. John Shea says that we need to tell our stories over and over again until we finally "get them right."

My sense of the goodness, the richness, and the strength that can be found in personal stories is a gift I received from a friend.

My earliest memories of him are of my sitting on his lap, listening to his stories. My most cherished gift, even today, is a book, a reminder of my happiness when this friend brought storybooks to me, books I could only hug when I was too young to read.

Recalling what I can about his stories brings back the qualities of both the story and the man. Remembering him and his stories gives me some insights into his life that I am sure I did not have as a child. Remembering the stories and the man is important because the stories I read now and the qualities I look for in friends are somehow related to him whose love for me challenges me to write my own story with love and care.

In the security of his arms, I listened to stories that were always open-ended and usually about doing good for others. Whether it was a big black bear, a little girl, or an Olympic runner, the principal figure was involved in doing something for someone else and often at the risk of losing something very important.

Sometimes the same stories were repeated over and over with only the change of one small part, which, of course, changed the ending. I could never persuade this storyteller to give me any hints about the ending. The fun of stories, he told me, was that you did not know the end at the beginning. But he also taught me that, if I noticed what the people in his stories were doing and how they were treating other people, I could get some hint of the ending.

When I was older, and still liked to sit on his lap and listen to his stories, he told me that in real life people are writing the end of their own stories at the beginning and all along the way.

So well were those stories told in my childhood that I see a relationship between them and the stories that are life-giving for me now. His gift was that, through his stories, he expanded not only my vision of life but also my heart and soul. It was a gift that he was not afraid to share his own story with me and to tell me about its sad or hurting places.

One of the challenges that we face is to continually find meaning in the ordinary and to discover new insights in old and oft-repeated truths. It is the uncommon gift of the artist as storyteller to lead us into some new or meaningful way of perceiving that at which we often look. We are not invited, necessarily, to look at new things so much as we are called to see the things at which we look, to see them with our hearts as well as with our eyes.

The storyteller, through whatever medium, continually re-creates the ability to see more life in the very process of risking the vision by sharing it with an other. The storyteller continually trades a personal talent in an unforeseen way because telling our stories can open us to the meaning of the story of another.

Through the artist's effort to frame human experience in words, he or she shares not only his or her own story but yours and mine. The artist as storyteller, in the act of articulating a story he or she knows or wishes to understand better, frees us to see our own stories more clearly and leads us to want to share what we see.

When I was young I did not realize how blessed I was to have grown up with an excitement about the goodness and value of stories. As a child it never occurred to me that there were children who did not have the gift of a storyteller in their lives.

I did not realize then, and I wish I did not know it to

be true now, that there are children who never have a friend in whose secure arms they can look unafraid at what is larger than or less than life, or to see life for what it is and what it can become.

How can a child fully comprehend an adult's sense of satisfaction in life, satisfaction told in countless ways through stories, satisfaction rooted in the conviction that life matters and makes sense when we seek to share with others every gift given to us? Even an adult might not understand a person who, like my friend, believed his life would have been worthwhile if only one person lived better because he shared what he had. Even an adult might not understand a person who believed that he ought never decide to close a door or refuse to open one until he had considered what might be on the other side.

My storytelling friend helped me to look up at the sky and, in his own way, to try to reach it. His was no small heart, no heart that refused to give or receive love. His was not a heart afraid of life. The missing finger on his right hand was a reminder of the stories he told me about working in a lumber camp when he was a young boy, his way of helping to support his family.

This storytelling friend, this man whose arms gave me both inner freedom and security, taught me much about life as I listened to his stories.

His were arms that set me free, even as a child. They were arms that held me tight and gave me the sense of being loved unconditionally. The securest place in the world for me as a child was in his arms. To be told another story was one of life's greatest gifts.

Because he taught me how it feels to be held by arms that are freeing, he calls me to a kind of accountability when my arms are not freeing for others. And, he calls me to an awareness of when the arms of others are not freeing for me.

I love this man. I remember him well. I still feel secure in his love. He was one of God's best gifts to my life. He is my father, the man I called "my daddy."

Privacy:
A Life-Giving Need
Secrecy: A Destructive Force

Directing conferences and retreat days over the past several years has put me in the position of being the one with whom many people have shared their stories, their lives, and, sometimes, their "secrets." It is an awesome experience to be invited into the lives of good people who are wrestling with the meaning of their unintended journeys, their finding themselves on an unanticipated or seemingly life-threatening path. The common feelings are fear, confusion, sadness, guilt, self-doubt. The common questions are: Can I survive this? What will others say? Will my friends be there for me? Do I have a future?

Listening carefully to their stories, their feelings, their questions, it has been my experience that two issues arise out of what is either an opportunity for greater, more faithful life or a place of necessary destruction and the loss of a possibility for future life.

The two issues that arise, which need to be separated and reflected upon, are those of privacy and secrecy. This task is not easy because the distinctions between the two are often subtle and because people often fail to acknowledge the right of grown-up, responsible men and women to make their own decisions without apology and without explanation. This is not to ignore the basic principles of sensitivity and personal accountability to those with whom we have shared life. Neither is it an invitation to the curious and the mean-spirited to prey on the growing edges of the lives of others.

There is a tendency for people to want to "unmask" others, to "get inside their heads," to persuade themselves that they have a right to know the deepest feelings of others.

Are we sometimes guilty of these tendencies because we are afraid to probe too deeply into our own feelings and inner motivations? Is it because we somehow want to skip some steps in figuring out our own lives by demanding the most intimate self-revelations of others? Sometimes others expect us to reveal our inner selves for their own unknown purposes. Often, lives are either sacrificed to or cut off by the probing focus of others, when rather what is needed is a private place in which to come to terms with one's own soul.

I was reminded of the issues of the differences between privacy and secrecy when I was directing a workshop for a large group of people. I had agreed to do the workshop with some reservations, having just been through one of the major and most costly transition times of my life.

Two or three days into that workshop, a young man sitting in the front row stopped my introductory presentation to say, "All this is inspiring and interesting, but we are waiting to hear your story."

Momentarily too stunned to find words, I quickly and instinctively realized that he was invading my privacy. His bold curiosity about my sacred inner space and personal journey was shocking.

This was a clarifying moment for me, one that I will not forget. It was my most dramatic venture into the meaning of and the necessity for privacy. His intrusiveness left me feeling violated. He simply had no right to ask, and certainly had no right to know. It had nothing to do with a right to "keep a secret"; it had everything to do with the life that emerges through privacy and the distortion that happens when persons are put in the position of believing that their only resort is secrecy. I believe that the need for secrecy is inherently destructive while the right to privacy offers the possibility of responsible searching for where life is or can be.

It is a fact of human life that we need time and space if we are to internalize values, discover meaning, distill the events of life that sometimes come at us too rapidly. We do not immediately make sense of things for ourselves, and, the larger the issue, the longer the process. When others place any kind of pressure on us to explain to them what we do not yet understand ourselves, when they refuse us the privacy that we need, or when they inject implications of certain guilt, we are denied the healthy, human way of responding faithfully to the surprising and costly moments of our lives.

The following experiences were shared with me, and I believe that each might have been different if undue outside pressures, in whatever way and from whatever source, had not been present.

▼ A young man is told that he cannot come home to join in the family Christmas celebration because his parents do not want to tell the other relatives that he is divorced.

▼ A young woman, pregnant and in high school, is sent to another part of the country to live with relatives until after the baby is born and put up for adoption.

▼ A man dies of AIDS, and when he is buried, two words never mentioned at any time around the memorial service and gathering are homosexual and AIDS. "Too bad that such a young person died of cancer," is all that is offered.

▼ Addictive families learn to "keep the secret" at the heart of the home until everyone in the family becomes as ill as the addicted one.

The most powerful words in Greg Louganis's book, *Breaking the Surface*, are the following, "Fear has ruled my life for too long, and I'm grateful to my family and the friends who protected me, but I don't need that kind of support anymore. To my family and friends, who already know much of what you are going to read about my life, I have a simple request: Don't protect me anymore. Don't keep my secrets anymore. Help me live my life openly and honestly."

His story tells the terrible price he paid for living a secret, and the lives of others make it clear that the distance between secrets and lies often cannot be distinguished.

When Arthur Ashe was forced to publicly share a truth from which he wanted to protect his daughter, Camera, he argued up to the final minutes that "the public has no right to know." Those in a position to make his decision for him disagreed without respect for his right to personal privacy.

In his book, *Soul Mates*, Thomas Moore, reflecting on the concepts of friendship and community, speaks of friendship's need for "containment," for the freedom of spirit required for mutuality and for the possibility of expanding life.

I share the belief with many others that much of what determines how or if life unfolds is related to whether or not we begin by asking life-giving questions. It makes all the difference if our driving force is related to our life-giving right to privacy or our fear-driven flight from life into secrecy. Much of this may be determined by whether we are directed from inside ourselves or whether we give those around us a power they may want but to which they have no right.

The question is not, "Who needs to know?" the

question is, "With whom would sharing this information be helpful and constructive to my life?"

The question is not, "If I tell someone will they try to change my mind?" the question is, "Who can I share this with who will offer support while I figure it out?"

The question is not, "Will someone find out?" the question is, "Will I live well with the decision I am making?"

Whatever the questions, there is little doubt that personal integrity and responsibility are jeopardized when we lack the time and space we need for life to take its own course, without a need to hurry or hide.

Golf and Other Soul-Expanders

It is a commonly accepted belief that "people grow and change when they become too uncomfortable to stay the way they are." My own version of this is that "necessity often pushes us where virtue never led us." At the heart of these statements is the conviction that, whether we like them or not, we do need some things in our lives that either haunt us or nudge us in such a way that we are challenged to examine either the way we are or the way we might dream of becoming. The writer Thomas Moore refers to this process as "soul making."

In recent years, I have unwittingly added some things to my life that have turned out to nudge and prod me in ways I could never have envisioned. In its own unique and very seductive way, the game of golf has proved to be closely related to how my soul has been made and, perhaps, needs to be re-made.

With the assistance of a patient and gifted teacher named Leonard, I know that I am learning to play the game. I also know that, in the hands of this same teacher and without his intent, every life issue with which I have ever struggled is played out in one way or another on what I have come to call "Heartbreak Hill," the place where I meet my teaching pro for lessons.

Golf is proving to be one of the places where my soul is revealed to me, or where I am reminded of many things I already know about myself. Sometimes my teacher feels more to me like a spiritual director or counselor than a conveyor of the techniques of this game.

When I made the decision to learn golf and took my first lesson two years ago, I had the same feeling expressed by W. Timothy Gallwey in *The Inner Game of Tennis* when he says, "Somehow, I sensed that, for me, golf could prove to be a dangerous game." Until now, achievement scores in negative numbers were unknown to me.

The "dangerous aspect" of the game is, for me, continually being confronted with and reminded of life issues with which I will wrestle as long as I live. They are woven into the fabric of me so tightly that we are "stuck" with one another. I wish it could be different, not just because I would like to be a shining star pupil in the school of golf, but because lifelong programming to make things come out right, to believe that the harder I work the better I will do, and a host of other such scripts interfere with my desire to live a more reasonably relaxed life. Golf reminds me of the unlearning that is between me and freedom.

When I make my best effort at a swing and miss the ball, my teacher smiles and says, "It happens to all of us." Inside of me I am thinking, "But it shouldn't if I worked at it harder." Life issues are just that, and I fear that they may outlive my time of golf lessons.

The point of this reflection is not to encourage others to follow me and/or Tiger into the mysterious and difficult game of golf. The point is that to remain faithful to our lives and to provide for both learning and unlearning, we need to choose some new arenas and explore some worlds different from those already familiar to us. In this way we can either expand our horizons or be reminded in undeniable ways of what we already know. Golf does both for me.

In addition to venturing into the world of golf, I spend Fridays at a shelter for battered women. The shelter work has been a part of my life for eight years now. For six years, I facilitated a group for children ages four to ten. My role now varies from spending time in court with women seeking restraining orders to cleaning shelter units and reading to children.

I wish everyone could live in a world free of violence. I had not realized how much young children are affected by what has gone on around them. My world grows larger as they share life with me.

A few weeks ago I was reading a book with four-year-old Eric. He seemed older to me as he told me his own story about each page as we went through the book. When we had completed the book, we decided to draw some pictures. After a short time, Eric gave me the picture he had drawn—a picture of a rabbit much like one we had seen in the book. As he pointed out the ears, the whiskers, and other typical rabbit characteristics, I noticed that the rabbit was holding an object that looked to me like a huge carrot. When I pointed to that place and asked Eric what the rabbit was holding, Eric looked up at me in surprise and said, "Paula, that is Rabbit's gun."

I have no idea what my face registered, but Eric quickly added, "Rabbit needs a gun to be safe, but Rabbit wouldn't hurt anyone." I was confronted with the sad truth that in this four-year-old's world, people believe they need guns.

In a very unpleasant way, Eric had pushed the margins of my thinking into the realm of worlds in which I have never lived and in which I wish no one else had to live.

The stories are countless, the issues are as varied as the lives of the people I meet at the shelter. I go there feeling that all I have to offer is the presence of a person who cares. I leave knowing that I am being changed and am cherished for the little that I can offer. The beautiful people I meet there make my world larger and my inner attitudes more flexible.

For several years, I became the gofer for an old man in a nursing home. When he needed stamps, toothpaste, shaving cream, Rolaids, or whatever, I brought them to room 305. When it was holiday time and his nurses needed to be thanked, I brought in trays of cookies and candy. When he sent me ten pounds of Vidalia onions each spring, they were returned to him in a wonderful French onion soup that he was treated to in small portions by the nurses who knew how much he loved it.

He lived for the football season, and I, who had not enough knowledge about the pro teams, learned about every team and the top players and knew the scores when I went to see him on Monday.

We were an unlikely set of friends because, as a matter of detail, he was the father of my husband's first wife. He seemed to make no judgments and accepted me from the beginning as the person who cared about him and would get his stamps and other necessary items there when he needed them. When his daughter, my husband's first wife, died, we were all he had.

But over the years, the love grew, and the time spent with him became more precious. His last birthday card to me said, "I could not love a daughter more."

My friend, Giff, opened so many worlds to me. But, most of all, this man who was in continual pain, confined to his bed, never complained, never put his burdens on anyone. Loving and gracious to the end, he taught me about worlds unknown to me. My parents died relatively young and at great distances from me. I always said that I wanted to be there for him in ways I could not be for my parents.

Born into a family of eight children—three boys and

five girls—I have often felt like we were a kind of mini-United Nations as we grew up.

I believe that my parents loved each other and all of us. I would never have thought of my world as being "limited." We moved often because of Daddy's job as a school superintendent. We had everything we needed but certainly not everything we wanted.

Siblings do fight and disagree, and a large family can be a superb leveling ground for any child who seems to depart too far from the family norms, spoken or unspoken.

For me to show up in my family, the third youngest having been the baby for five years, as the one who stayed out later than the agreed time, had wilder, noisier friends, set my siblings insisting that my parents rein me in, demand that I be home earlier, and, generally, that they take charge of this wild kid.

I remember resenting everything they ever told my parents, but we loved each other, and our world started out larger than most children in this era will ever know.

There are many ways in which to expand our worlds. There are different possibilities for pushing us beyond us where we are. None of this happens easily, and it does not happen pain-free.

Soul-expanders are all around us; some are obvious and intrusive, others are not. To discover the wider perimeters of our lives, we may have to exchange life-long ways of doing and thinking for ways that are foreign and, therefore, frightening.

For a Dollar and My Umbrella: The Art of Making a Deal

The work of Dr. Elizabeth Kubler-Ross in helping establish a useful framework in which to articulate the implications of death and dying was a monumental contribution to our world community. Like her, others in the late 1960s, including Dr. John Brantner at the University of Minnesota, were channels of healing and hope for all of us.

In discussing five stages of grieving and the process itself, we had an opportunity to find meaning in Kubler-Ross's words that went far beyond death and dying. It was around that time that people working with the divorce adjustment process saw and claimed the parallels between the stages of grieving for the dying and for those divorcing.

One of the stages in the process was named "bargaining." We had all known the meaning of making a bargain, working out economic arrangements to the satisfaction of both parties involved. What most of us had never done was to identify and articulate other applications of that term which we were already using in trying to make our lives more manageable or more comfortable. One such example: "If I make good decisions and work hard, my life will work out according to plan."

THE LITTLE BOY AND HIS PROPOSED BARGAIN

My awareness of the meaning of making a bargain was heightened through a five-year-old friend named Kevin.

Kevin was often standing on the corner outside the neighborhood butcher shop when I visited there almost every Saturday morning. He manifested more than a small amount of interest in my car, a red Miata convertible. Each Saturday he would have some new question for me, including how to open the ragtop cover, and if he could have a ride. I showed him how easily the cover could be put back and explained to him that I could only give him a ride if he could bring his mother there to talk with me.

On this particular Saturday, it had been raining. When I walked from my Miata to the door of the butcher shop, Kevin approached me with some excitement as he said, "If I give you a dollar and my umbrella, do you think we could trade your car for my mother's car?" When I again told him that this deal would have to involve his mother, he explained to me that she was at work.

As I think about little Kevin and his proposed deal, my thoughts turn to the art of bargaining and the many applications and implications of the process. I am drawn to ask such questions as: Why do we bargain? When do we bargain? With whom do we bargain? It is clear to me that the circumstances under which people bargain may vary and are sometimes related to misconceptions that have a profound impact on our lives. Some of these misconceptions may develop as responses to frustrating situations.

STATEMENTS I HAVE FREQUENTLY HEARD

"My husband has cancer. I believe that, if I go to Mass every day and make a novena, God will find a cure for him."

"If I marry a Catholic instead of the Protestant I love, I believe that I will never have to worry about a divorce."

"If I make an effort to live well and do good things for others, I believe that bad things will happen neither to me nor to my children."

"I have not always been honest in my business dealings, and I believe that if I give money to charity everything will work out for me."

"If I try hard enough, I believe that I will always succeed at whatever I choose to do."

COMMON MISCONCEPTIONS RELATED TO THESE STATEMENTS

Misconceptions about God. It is not uncommon for God to be thought of as some sort of universal dispenser of all good things. It is as though we expect that, in exchange for prayers, good deeds, and promises to repent, God will automatically respond according to our plans and demands.

Misconceptions about the meaning of prayer. By quoting the biblical passage, "Ask and you shall receive," prayer is sometimes perceived as an automatic guarantee that we will receive, in a fairly effortless way, whatever it is that we are presently demanding. Or, we believe that we can use it to change God's mind. The truth is that prayer can change the pray-er, that inner attitudes can be transformed, but prayer is not like a supply on demand situation.

Misconceptions about sin. When we own our deliberate sins, good things can happen for us. Our sin does not diminish God, does not make God less. It is ourselves that we harm by choosing that which makes us less than we might have been. It is ourselves that we harm each time we choose evil over good.

Misconceptions about the words "Be ye perfect." Only one is perfect or ever can be—God. For the rest of us, doing our human best is our way of being called to the fullest possible life. Accepting our human imperfections is at the heart of the Christian call to follow the human Jesus as we struggle with the reality of being less than perfect.

Misconceptions about the source of our countless forms of guilt. In his book *How Good Do We Have to Be?*, Harold Kushner gives us a powerful reminder of just how destructive it can be to the lives of good people if they continue to define themselves by their worst moments instead of the best ones, carrying myriad forms of guilt that haunt and rob good people of valuable energy for renewed life. There are many times we have allowed ourselves or others to persuade us that God is like a Divine Accountant, lying in wait to trip us up.

These and other misconceptions about the meaning of human life and the loving Creator of that life can lead us to undue preoccupation with striking some sort of deal that will keep us forever free of pain, failure, disappointment, frustration, tragedy, and all forms of loss and discomfort.

It is a very human thing to try whatever we can that will, we hope, gain for us whatever it is we believe we need or want. How often have we come before a loving God just like little Kevin, offering "a dollar and our umbrella" in order to get what we believe we need or to avoid what we fear will cause us unspeakable pain?

Jesus was not beyond trying to make a deal with God: "Father, if it be possible, can we arrange to do this another way?" Perhaps we experience some sort of relief from our fears and concerns simply by verbalizing what it is that is causing the anguish.

WHEN DO WE GET INVOLVED IN BARGAINING?

In its definitions of *bargain*, the dictionary refers to an agreement that has worth to two parties, to a discussion that is in search of the best possible terms for both, to arriving at some form of mutual satisfaction.

Reflecting on when we enter into the process of bargaining we may discover that we may be dealing with various forms of fear: fear of risking, fear of inevitable pain, fear of the loss of control, fear of being forced beyond our own comfort limits. Whatever the process involves for each of us, when we find ourselves planning our next negotiation, we might remind ourselves that we cannot effectively short-circuit life. Things work out for the best when they are allowed to take their normal course. When dealing with things outside of ourselves, striking the deal we want may prove fruitful. When we are dealing in the realm of inner geography, few things will free us more quickly from our stuck places and move us more effectively along on our inward journey than putting aside all bargaining and simply choosing to do the very things we fear.

Home Is Not a Place

Home is a holy thing—nothing of doubt or distrust can enter its blessed portals . . . Here seems indeed to be a bit of Eden which not the sin of any can utterly destroy.

▼ EMILY DICKINSON

The word home may be one of the richest in the human language in terms of its ability to evoke feelings and memories. The wise and the simple, the poet and the playwright, the child and the grownup respond to the word *home*.

Robert Frost spoke of it as a place "which, when you go there, they have to take you in." He added that it is also a place we ought never have to deserve.

T. S. Eliot says that "home is where one starts." It represents to him a place of origin and a place to which one can return to discover new meaning.

Thomas Moore, in his book *Re-Enchantment*, speaks of the soulfulness of our sense of home and the "enchantment that home can bring into a life." He adds that it will not be and need not be a perfect place.

The Israelites groaned and cried out in anguish because of their slavery and their longing for home (Ex 2:23-25).

ET, the extra-terrestrial, revealed a longing for his own land when he continually expressed his need and desire to "phone home."

Emily Dickinson reminds us of the feelings of acceptance and security we have when we are going home when she said, "For you know we do not mind our dress, When we are going home."

Warriors of all ages, through their speech and writing, reflect not only the agony of war but the longing for home.

It is not uncommon for people to be in their own house with family and friends and yet not feel *at home*. It is also possible to be among strangers in a foreign land and feel *at home*, comfortable, accepted.

HOME AND HOMELESSNESS

The plight of the homeless in cities and countries all over the world has given great visibility to the meaning of home. We are all too aware that there are forms of homelessness that have little or nothing to do with houses. Some forms of homelessness are not easily defined, nor are they easily healed. Life circumstances sometimes leave people feeling homeless, isolated, unsupported, and hopeless. Included among these homeless are the following:

- ▼ People who feel separated from others by barriers of color, language, sex, sexual orientation, or religious conviction.
- ▼ People who live too far below the poverty level to be able to feel a sense of belonging to any kind of community.
- ▼ Teenagers who struggle with inner turmoil and/or personal issues that confuse them and that they are afraid to share.
- ▼ Families that are caught in the secrets and lies involved with the myriad forms of addiction which destroy the possibility of any kind of healthy relationship.
- ▼ The wealthy who feel exploited by the ever-present demands of others, and the famous who long for the privacy usually associated with being at home.

One of the great mysteries related to the concept of home is that no other person can "give us a home" because being at home demands various forms of exchange, mutuality, interplay, and self-involvement. Our feelings are the clearest gauge of whether or not we are *at home*.

The dictionary says that home is "the place where a person lives," "the place where one was born and reared," "the place where something has been originated/developed." None of these touches on a common human longing to be where we know that someone cares, that there is a place where we are cherished and loved for who we are.

The dictionary does not reveal the "soulful" dimension of home. The descriptions do not tell us that if no one can give us the fullness of home, so neither can anyone ever really take that sense of home away from us once we have had it.

The inner dimensions of home not revealed by the dictionary include:

▼ A feeling of security. When we are at home, we feel safe in the belief that who we are is respected and cared about.

▼ A feeling of acceptance. It was this dimension of home I believe Robert Frost was referring to when he said that home was a place we would never have to "deserve." Good behavior will not earn it and mistakes will not cause it to be lost.

▼ A belief that we do not have to be perfect. When we are at home, we can relax into the human condition into which we are all born. We accept our gifts and our limitations with equal ease.

▼ A sense of mutuality, of give and take. We need not concern ourselves with measuring and weighing, but rather with the gentle art of giving and receiving with equal ease.

▼ Feelings of vulnerability which are neither feared nor denied. By sharing our very fragile feelings, we find the most profound trust and openness.

▼ A courage to face our fears. When we are at home, in an environment of respect and acceptance, we see more clearly and are able to gain perspective and courage for whatever lies ahead.

In considering these feelings and the many others unnamed, I am haunted by hundreds of children I have met who have not experienced what Thomas Moore speaks of in his book *Re-Enchantment* when he says, "Home is a place in the imagination where feelings of security, belonging, placement, family, protection, memory and personal history abide. Our dreams and fantasies of home give us direction and calm our anxieties as we continually look for ways to satisfy our longings for home."

In addition to these children, I think about people who, lacking relationship skills and a healthy sense of themselves, without realizing what they are doing, give themselves away to gain the acceptance of others. In so doing, they are giving away whatever of *home* may reside in their hearts. Allowing another person to occupy all of our inner space removes from us the possibility of ever having all the wonderful and life-giving feelings associated with being at home.

Home is clearly not a place. Home is a set of feelings

and inner attitudes out of which arises the general sense of rootednees and well-being. It begins with our ability to feel at home with ourselves and flows out from there to reach into the lives of others to offer them a sense of being at home. We know when we are at home. We also know when others are able to feel at home in our friendship and presence.

I return to the opening quotation from Emily Dickinson:

> Home is a holy thing—nothing of doubt or distrust can enter its blessed portals.

Small Gifts: Giant Treasures

. . . The wise man looks into space, and does not regard the small as too little, nor the great as too big: for he knows there is no limit to dimensions.

▼ LAO TSE

The faithful person internalizes and holds close those things and events that are perceived to have value. Things and events make a deep impression because they have values, they are beautiful, and they are filled with goodness and the truth of life.

If we have not trained our heart's eye to notice the small treasure, we may miss the meaning of life's more important events. If we miss the energy in the easy-to-ignore, how can we hope to celebrate the obvious?

Life passes by us, most often, in small irretrievable increments. Our minds and our culture program us to expect life in the large, the dramatic, the undeniably meaningful event. Sometimes, it is there—the unexpected success or promotion that calls for celebration, or the event that captures our imagination and our emotions. And, like all of creation, we recognize that this is good.

While celebrating life's wondrously mysterious moments of grandeur, it is important to remember that the mark of the truly great is to acknowledge the seemingly unimportant, the event nearly too small to notice.

Life's heart, life's hope is built, like a wall, stone by stone, precious piece by precious piece. Building hope and heart is a process; it is not an event.

Every human life is a series of events, a series of places we have journeyed, persons we have met. Every human life is also a series of decisions made, doubts overcome, rejections faced, losses counted and put behind.

Whether these are small or large, the thoughtful, self-reflective person begins to notice and value every sign of life, sometimes hidden and sometimes obvious, sometimes nearly overwhelming and sometimes nearly uneventful.

In Thornton Wilder's play *Our Town*, Emily poses a question to each of us, "Does any human being ever realize life while they live it—every, every minute?" While there is no simple answer to that question, there are some choices we can make that may ensure our ability to respond with more frequency.

One important choice we can make is to stop looking for the easy life that we hope will be present in the signs and wonders that may occasionally appear. Most of life is not experienced in that way. Until we accept that truth, we will be confronted with unnecessary disappointment and frustration.

In David Mamet's play *Speed the Plow*, I found some words both insightful and comforting: ". . . but it was not an accident. That I came here. Sometimes it reaches for us. And we say, 'Show me a sign.' And when it reaches us, then we see we *are the sign*. And we find the answers."

Because every human life is sacred, every event that is a part of that life carries a kind of often unacknowledged importance. The fact is, each life event has meaning. There really are no "small events" as there are no "small gifts."

The poet William Blake talks about "seeing a world in a grain of sand." The artist Georgia O'Keefe says, "nobody sees a flower, really—it is so small—we haven't time, and, to see takes time, like to have a friend takes time."

Tennyson gives great respect to the small flower when he writes, "Flower in the crannied wall, I pluck you out of the crannies, I hold you here—root and all, in my hand. . . . Little flower . . . ."

At workshops and on retreat weekends, when I ask people what sustains them on a day-to-day basis, they speak of the clerk in the grocery store who smiled and took time to ask them how they were; the friend who took time to write a note to thank or to share; the family member who said, "I'm sorry. Please forgive me"; the surprise visit from someone who brings smiles and laughter; the words "Good job" from a coworker; the strong handshake that shows connection and care; the phone call that says simply, "Just called to let you know that I am thinking about you and sending love"; a person who pays attention by looking into your eyes when he or she talks to you. These, and countless other seemingly unimportant manifestations of care, are what people who manifest a desire to grow beyond where they are continually tell me has made the difference for them. On a day-to-day basis, it is the accumulation of seemingly insignificant gifts that has the sustaining power for which people speak countless words of gratitude.

We cannot afford to expect all of life to come to us in large and dramatic events, however welcome these are when they occur. There is no substitute for cultivating a way of life that cherishes small blessings and can be excited in relationship to things that all too often go unnoticed. In his letter to the Colossians, St. Paul says, "Dedicate yourselves to thankfulness" (Col 3:17). He does not say that gratitude comes instinctively. It is as though he is saying, "If you want to experience the best of life, make a commitment to expressing thanks for each good gift that comes your way."

I read recently that it is important to plan our day in

such a way that we have something to which we really look forward, something, however seemingly unimportant, to which we can look as a source of joy.

My old friend named Giff, confined to his bed in a nursing home, told me that each morning he awaited daylight so he could watch the pigeons on a telephone wire outside his only window. He got joy out of watching them and their arrangements in relation to each other. While it did not equal his love for Monday night football, it was not unimportant.

Over the years, Giff told me about other special sources of joy for him. He was, for me, not only a friend but also a role model for how to face the final years.

In our complex world of multi-national corporations, world banks, worldwide web sites, and Internet links, it is all too easy to discount the value of the small and undramatic.

We have choices to make. We can refuse to let our lives happen without us. We can look more carefully, listen with greater sensitivity, and receive graciously the richness that is a part of every day. But, most important of all, we must be prepared for, or at least be open to, the life that comes to us out of the nearly unacknowledged, because "too small" gifts will be there as surely as the pigeons return to the telephone wires outside Giff's room.

The sources of the tenderness that beautifies and the gift that radiates warmth make their impact felt:

I came to buy a smile—today—
But just a single smile—
The smallest one upon your face
Will suit me just as well—
The one that no one else would miss
It shone so very small—
I'm pleading at the "counter" sir—
Could you afford to sell—

Say—may I have it—Sir?

▼ EMILY DICKINSON

Mixed Blessings: Each One Is

Precisely because death awaits us in the end,
we must live fully. Precisely because an event
seems devoid of meaning, we must give it one.
Precisely because the future eludes us, we must
create it.

▼ ELIE WIESEL, MEMOIRS

One of the most certain things about human life is its lack of clarity. One of the most fearsome things about human life is the disturbing presence of tensions that invite us to a deeper level of meaning. One of the ever-present realities of human life is our desire for certainty, our overriding hope that we can avoid the possible error associated with risk. We grow weary of the array of contradictions that seem to surround us and pursue us.

We long for the kind of security that we hope to find in some sourcebook (perhaps the Bible); we seek out a guru or spiritual director who can help untangle the confusing threads and bring wisdom and light. We do this even though we know, at least intellectually, that the beauty and richness of life are discovered in the subtler colors and deeper hues which are mingled among the brighter hues in the tapestry of life.

When we take time to reflect upon the events of our lives we give credence to the belief that every blessing, however large or small, is a mixture of gift and challenge. We somehow know that life's contradictions have a power to reveal what we could learn in no other way. We recognize that life without risk cannot lead us to greater life.

> You risked your life, but what else have you ever risked? Have you ever risked disapproval? Have you ever risked a belief? . . . Real courage is in risking something you have to keep on living with, real courage is risking something that might force you to rethink your thoughts and suffer change and stretch consciousness . . .
>
> ▼ TOM ROBBINS,
> *ANOTHER ROADSIDE*
> *ATTRACTION*

I know of no person whose life has gone "according to plan." Whether in relationship to events large or small, decisions important or of less magnitude, the most frequent comments are:

"I was not prepared for this."

"I never dreamed this could happen to us."

"I am a college graduate, highly trained and skilled. I never expected to be jobless."

"We would never have believed this could happen to a child of ours."

"Pregnant! Not my seventeen-year-old daughter."

"Divorce! Not in our faithful family."

"My son would never use drugs."

The list could be much longer. The details could be much more varied. But, with this list we are yet confronted with the truth, the often pain-filled reality of life's unintended journeys. Life's unpredicted happenings and contradictions respect neither age nor position, economic status nor power, faithfulness to life nor refusal to believe. Life's blessings and its mysterious intrusions will, at some time or another, become our companions on what once seemed to be a certain and predicted way.

It is not so much the happenings as our response to them that will determine whether these are moments of grace or dead-end obstructions. Our thoughts and our periods of self-reflection carry the power to determine how we respond, how we treat other people, how we treat ourselves. In our chosen response is the transforming gift and the ability to overcome any obstacle. It makes a difference how we view, believe, and think about crisis times. It makes a difference whether we see both opportunity and danger; it makes a difference whether or not we accept what we cannot change.

Life's greatest blessings are often masked; limitations are sometimes the only key to meaning. I was reminded of this when I reread the words of Earl Charles Spencer when he spoke of Princess Diana in these words, "Diana remained a very insecure person at heart, almost childlike in her desire to do good for others so she could release herself from deep feelings of unworthiness. The world cherished her vulnerability. . . ."

A friend said it in another way on the occasion of the death of John Denver when he said, "In mourning his passing we can all appreciate what he left behind. Like the rest of us, he was human but was able to share a wonderful gift with the world. We are all better off for his having lived."

In the end, the lives of others can reveal to us that no life need be lived perfectly, and no limitation is, of itself, a diminishing factor in any human life. The destruction seems to happen when, for whatever reason, we feel a need to go to great lengths to hide from one another lest we be unmasked in some manner that is not respectful of the sacredness of each human life.

It is a sometimes unsettling truth to acknowledge and accept the fact that *life is not fair*. Good people do suffer and lose while bad people seem free and prosperous. What once may have seemed like a great blessing in our lives may, one day, become a place of pain. What was once viewed as a great gift in someone's life may, one day, be the cause of that person's undoing. Sometimes life is about letting go and moving on. Sometimes we have to unlearn and learn again. It makes all the difference how we look at things; it matters if we are able to turn things over in our minds so that we can acknowledge both sides of a single reality.

MIXED BLESSINGS: TREASURES WITH OPPOSITE FACES

▼ Love is about being with; it is about companionship and presence. Yet, it is impossible to have love without the possibility of its loss.

▼ Self-revelation and vulnerability are at the heart of relationship. Yet to open the heart in this way is to be open to great emotional risk.

▼ To be a comfort-bearer to others is a place of life for both the giver and the receiver. Yet, in the process of being present to the circumstances of the life of another often places us is a position of great discomfort.

▼ To be open to and to receive new life in any form is an act of courage. Yet it asks of us the willingness to let go of what is no longer life-giving, no matter the degree of attachment we have had.

▼ Human suffering is not, of itself, destructive of life. Pain is inevitable, growth is optional. Yet, to choose life can be as frightening as it is energizing.

▼ St. Paul, wrestling with the lack of clarity that is a part of life, said, "At present we see indistinctly, as in a mirror." We are not often comfortable with this obscured vision of what lies ahead. Yet, having feared the darkness, sometimes we come to a place where we see clearly what life demands of us, and we are even more uncomfortable.

▼ Carl Jung said that "the soul resides in the valleys of life and not on the peaks of the intellectual." Yet, we somehow do not expect to discover meaningful life in the undramatic places.

▼ Every person needs carefully set inner boundaries—the spaces where we own our own souls. Yet, the refusal to establish inner boundaries may be the greatest obstacle to determining where the outer boundaries, between ourselves and others, are life-giving and where they are destructive to our ability to relate to others. The poet Ranier Maria Rilke wrote eloquently of his belief that, in relationship, two separate selves meet and care for one another.

There is no limit to the illustrations we might use to establish the dual nature of every gift—part pleasing and part prodding. Sets of opposing forces in human life shape us—inner and outer forces. And, in the tension where these two sets of forces interface is the sacred space where new life comes to be. The desire in us for freedom from this tension and the discomfort it brings with it often leads us to try to find ways to rid ourselves of its gnawing presence.

We may be most human and alive when we operate

not out of certainty and clarity, but out of uncertainty and doubt. Almost all of life's greatest treasures are partnered with something that has potential for destroying as well as building: love and rejection, joy and sadness, success and failure.

The poet Edna St. Vincent Millay expresses it this way:

> Water, is taught by thirst.
> Land—by oceans passed.
> Transport—by throe—
> Peace—by its battles told—
> Love, by Memorial Mold—
> Birds, by the snow.

Laughter, The Liberator

Nothing connects me with a person quicker than knowing what he laughs at. Nothing is more valuable in a relationship than loose and easy laughter.

I know no wiser words than the stainless steel truth that he who laughs, lasts.

▼ ROBERT FULGHUM,
WORDS I WISH I WROTE

The power of laughter is unique. When it is spontaneous, it is at once free and freeing. It can lift the spirits not only of the one laughing but of all who are present to see and hear. We identify laughter with a sense of celebration. It is an indicator that all is right within the soul of the one who laughs.

In a book called *I Am Not a Crybaby*, Helen Cogancherry describes the many occasions on which we are released from the burden of buried feelings by crying. My father used to say that tears are like drops of holy water, washing us out inside so that we can see more clearly. We cry at births and deaths, at times of separation and of reuniting. Tears come with equal ease when we are hurting and when we are happy, something that is not always true of laughter.

Laughter, when it is effortless and spontaneous, is both freeing and contagious. There is also a time when laughter is strained and binding. There is a kind of humor and laughter that can distance people from one another rather than connecting them.

It has long been the role of the clown to facilitate laughter. Robert Speaight, in *The Book of Clowns*, says that "the jester represented a safety-valve in feudal society," and George Bishop in *The World of Clowns* says of laughter: "While it surely will not solve the world's problems it provides us all with a means of relieving tension" (p. xi). Laughter has its own way of keeping us in touch with reality by refusing to let us become over-burdened with the sadness and tragedy that are an inevitable part of every human life.

In her book *The Space Between Us*, Ruthellen Josselson reminds us that laughing together is one of the great joys and pleasures in life. Sharing laughter heightens its importance in the lives of friends. Laughing and playing together is one of the greatest antidotes to the overly serious way in which we sometimes present ourselves even to those who are very close to us.

When Pope John Paul I gave the world a marvelous gift in his volume of letters called *Illustrissimi*, those who read his letters to Mark Twain, Charles Peguy, Hippocrates, and Pinocchio recognized an unusual and refreshing quality that our world today badly needs. It was said of him, "Cardinal Luciani arises as an enemy of boredom. . . ."

Thomas Moore in *Soul Mates* speaks of humor and wit, the companions of laughter, as "signs of soulfulness." He says of humor that it "can be defined in part as an enjoying of a multiple viewpoint, so that even tragic and unhappy events can be seen from another angle, liberating us from "the tyranny of narrow vision."

Because laughter is so essential to the complete life of the human spirit, it is important for reasonable people to identify ways in which they can liberate themselves from a narrow vision and discover the joy that is hidden away in a variety of places.

One sure place of freedom and openness to greater life is in stories. A great resource for altering life's too serious moments can be found in the power of stories that tickle the human spirit and bring joy. While these stories may not necessarily make us laugh, they do prepare us for laughter by their ability to refocus that which feels heavy and downspirited.

The following stories never fail to bring that kind of joy both to me and to my listeners at conferences and workshops. I encourage everyone either to begin or to continue to develop such a resource.

IT'S A BABY CAR

One source of fun and playfulness in my life is my car—a red Miata convertible with a black ragtop. In addition to the feeling I have when I drive it that I am again sixteen years old, it continually attracts young children who gather around it in the parking lot outside the grocery store. Because it is so small (a friend of our son's calls it my "matchbox car"), children approach it as though they believe that they could just hop in and drive it away. One little boy stands beside it and pets it as though it were a puppy.

One day, I was giving two little girls a ride to a birthday party. When we arrived at the home of the second girl, she came out of her house and ran toward my car. She called out to her mother, "Look, Mommy. I think this car was just born. It's a baby car."

FIVE BOOKS AT A TIME

Having just paid ten dollars in library fines, my friend Rhonda was resolved that Hennessy, her eight-year-old daughter needed some guidelines. Being reluctant to in any way curtail her daughter's enthusiasm for reading (Rhonda is certain that Hennessy has read every book she has ever brought home from the library), the instruction to Hennessy as we entered the library was, "Five books at a time from now on. You cannot check out more than five books each time."

Having completed the book search, as we were leaving the library, Rhonda noticed that Hennessey's backpack was bulging. When she was questioned about the number of books, the creative child's response was straightforward and nondefensive. She said, "I have twenty books, but I did as you asked—I checked them out five at a time."

Smiling at the undaunted and creative spirit of this eight-year-old, her mother, knowing my great love for Hennessy said to me, "Aren't you glad she is *my* daughter!"

TRICKY GUY

The mysteries of Holy Week and Easter are sometimes nearly incomprehensible to adults. A friend of mine decided that each day of Holy Week he would explain to his five-year-old son Ben what significance that day's events had in the life of Jesus. The meaning of Holy Thursday and the sharing of a parting meal with friends posed no problems. The events of Good Friday, the rejection of friends and the bitterness of enemies somehow seemed to fit with some elements of a child's young experience. Having described the burial of Jesus, the anointing by friends, and the setting of the guard left Ben with questions about the recent death of a grandparent.

As the story of Easter Sunday, the friends returning to the burial place of Jesus, was completed, my friend said, "Ben, when they rolled back the stone and looked inside for Jesus, the body of Jesus was gone. Jesus was not there." He waited for some moments before asking, "So what do you think about that, Ben?" He looked at his daddy, thought carefully, and then proclaimed, "I think Jesus was a tricky guy."

BEND YO BODY

Working in a summer program in Chicago proved to be one of my primary educational experiences. The participants were junior high school age girls who lived in the Chicago ghettos. It was hoped that the weeks they spent with us would help prepare them for high school. I learned two things in that time. First, that living where they did was mainly a survival experience. Second, I learned how to dance—more or less.

During one of our afternoon breaks, there was time for either volleyball or dancing. Having grown up as a kid who hated recess because I lacked athletic ability and was never chosen for any team, I asked if I could supervise the dancing.

What I observed, set to music, was something of a gymnastic wonder. These girls knew how to dance!

Soon I found myself invited to join them, and a bubbly sixth-grader volunteered to teach me. After several minutes, I assessed my progress as a C+. My partner was not so generous as she looked up at me, hands on her hips, and said, "What's the matter with you? You hurt somewhere?" As if that were not enough, she added, "Can't you bend yo body nohow?"

In my state of shock and disappointment I said something that I am certain meant nothing to my young listener. Trying to hide my disappointment, I said, "Look! I was trained in a very strict novitiate where they tried to persuade me that I didn't even have a body, and it's a little difficult to figure out where to bend it."

LET'S ELOPE

I was visiting at the home of friends following the sudden and heartbreaking death of a young mother of five children. Seeing the grief written large on every family member's face was painful. My own sadness left me caring yet wordless. I suspect that every pillow in that house was tear-stained at night.

We attended Mass on Sunday morning. I have no idea what was being said from the pulpit, but I was very aware of eight-year-old Steven, one of the children, who was sitting next to me.

He tugged on my sleeve, winked, and said, "Hey, Paula, let's elope." I couldn't believe what I had heard, and he read my surprise accurately as he went on to add, "Don't worry. It'll be okay. I have money. How about Hawaii?"

In the midst of such sadness, the humor in all of this was a welcome and healing moment for me. Steven seemed to understand that his playfulness would not be lost on me.

My friends recognize me as a very serious person. They acknowledge the presence in me of a good sense of humor, but often the serious side wins the day. When I suggested to someone that I might take a course on learning to play and be funny, her response was that I would probably take the course as seriously as I do everything else so that it might not be worth the effort.

Whatever the past assessments, I am learning, even if reluctantly. I agree with the profound words of James Thurber:

> After a little of Einstein, there ought to be a little of Cole Porter, after a talk about Kierkegaard and Kafka should come some imitations of Ed Wynn and Fields.
>
> Humor is counterbalance. Laughter need not be cut out of anything since it improves everything.
>
> The power that created the poodle, the platypus, and people has an integrated sense of both comedy and tragedy.

PAULA RIPPLE COMIN

brings a wealth of experience to her writing. She is a former college teacher and dean of students, and was the first executive director of the North American Conference of Separated and Divorced Catholics. She also worked for eight years with the children at shelters for battered women in LaCrosse, Wisconsin, and Naples, Florida. Since 1992 she has been presenting workshops and retreats throughout the United States and Canada for Retreats International Summer Institute for Retreat and Pastoral Ministry. Her previous books include *The Pain and the Possibility*, *Called to Be Friends*, *Walking With Loneliness*, and *Growing Strong at Broken Places* (all published by Ave Maria Press).